Sir Thomas Lipton Wins

Sir Thomas Lipton Wins

GEOFFREY WILLIAMS

PETER DAVIES : LONDON

797·14 /471972

Made and printed in Great Britain
by Morrison and Gibb Ltd., London and Edinburgh

For Robert Clark

Contents

Illustrations

Endpapers: Track charts for *Sir Thomas Lipton*, *Voortrekker*, *Cheers*, *Spirit of Cutty Sark* and *Raph*.

I

Wanting to Cruise

'Forasmuch as it hath pleased Almighty God of his great mercy to take unto himself the soul of our dear sister here departed, we therefore commit her body to the ground: earth to earth, ashes to ashes, dust to dust.'

My mother had died after a nine-month struggle against cancer. I can easily remember trying to restrain my tears as I walked down the gravel path and away from the grave. The cemetery was in a village near Redruth and it looked out over the North Cliffs and the sea. It was late in May and a brisk north-west wind gave the day a special clarity and painted the sky, sea, hills and fields in the bright colours of a child's picture book. I still associate this weather with the funeral and the north-west wind still leaves me full of apprehension and foreboding.

After the funeral I changed out of my stiff, best clothes and slipped out of the back door with my bicycle. It was a rather pedestrian, black bicycle which made hard work of the Cornish hills, but it had given me great pleasure during the last three years which I had spent exploring the countryside around Redruth. Recently, I had discovered a deep hidden pool cut out of granite by the Kennal river. It was near the village of Ponsanooth and I decided to return to this secret place today. As usual I was alone and wearing my school cap. A mixture of pride at getting into the local grammar school and a fear of falling foul of the custodians of the school rules made me very strict about wearing my school cap.

I

I left my bicycle chained to a tree near the main road and pushed through the dense undergrowth. After about a hundred yards the track opened out into a wooded amphitheatre whose stage was a crystal clear cistern continually flushed by the small Kennal river. It had just rained. As the wind rustled the trees a shower of droplets splashed on to the clean granite and into the liquid glass of the pool. I found a sheltered spot in some particularly dense undergrowth and took off my clothes. The brambles which had torn at my shirt on the way into the hideout tore at me on the way out and I cut myself again as I slid down the steep slabs of rock. The shock of the cold water closed the wounds and I watched, fascinated, as the blood dissolved and disappeared in the chuckling stream. The stronger gusts of wind parted the canopy of trees to let in the spring sunshine which glistened on the wet, new leaves and threw flashes of light across the water. By jumping up and down I could make the water rise up the massive granite walls, and if I was lucky the water would be draining down the crystals of quartz just as a beam of sunshine flashed by and the reflection would momentarily flood the underside of the leaves with a dazzling light.

I stayed in the icy water for a long time, reflecting on the events of the past few weeks and on my new-found situation. In that pool my body was shocked, cold and exposed in the same way that my mind had been since my mother's death became inevitable two weeks previously. When I could stand the cold no more I climbed warily to my makeshift bathing machine, dried myself with my handkerchief and warmed my body by pedalling furiously towards Redruth. Halfway up Pengreep Hill my muddled thoughts came together and my fifteen-year-old philosophy concluded that it was no use relying on other people if they were going to be taken away in this cruel fashion. But the injury went deeper and so must the remedy. The antidote called for a massive

show of independence. At this stage the form of the remedy w
unclear, and later, when a long singlehanded passage was deeme
to be the right medicine, the reasons for taking it had becom
diffuse and complicated.

Until I was seventeen everything I knew of the sea frightened
me. Redruth is four miles from the north coast of Cornwall and
ten miles from the south coast. The limited range of my black
bicycle gave me an intimate knowledge of the wild Atlantic coast
while the Channel shores remained a mystery. The coastline
between Newquay and St. Ives that I came to know so well must
rank as the most magnificent, yet inhospitable in all of England.
It is here that the three hundred foot platform land of north
Cornwall falls abruptly into the open Atlantic. There are no safe
harbours, no sheltered bays along the coast, and I have never seen
a sailing boat venture along this lee shore. A calm day is rare. The
wind blows incessantly from the west, howling up and over the
cliffs, delighting the seabirds which frolic in the updraughts and
the sailplanes that try to emulate them, driving waves ceaselessly
against the cliffs and beaches, providing endless entertainment for
the seals and the surfboard riders. We all knew the power of these
waves for each one of us at school had at one time or another been
lifted onto their crest, rushed down their tumbling front and had
the air blown out of our lungs as we crashed on to the hard-packed
sand. The continuous noise of the wind and the surf gave the scene
a sense of drama which all too often was justified. Each year a
number of people were drowned and others killed by falling
from the cliffs. The surf life-saving clubs were heavily subscribed,
but sailing was something that other people did.

Redruth owed its existence to the copper and tin mining
activities which reached their height in the middle of the last
century, but which are now represented by a single working
mine. The whole district seemed to have an understandable

distrust of the sea. Too often we had heard about the brave work of the St. Ives lifeboat. Too often we had lain awake in our warm beds hearing the wind and rain beat against the windows and thanking God that we were not 'out there'. During the last century the Cornish seafaring folk were smugglers, wreckers or fishermen. How futile it must have seemed to the people of this district to try to work *with* the sea in fishing or smuggling; how much easier it would be to lend a hand to its already powerful wrecking ability.

At school I was very conscious of the weather. From the school fields there was an uninterrupted view out to the North Cliffs and along the coast as far as St. Ives and Penwith. A corollary of being able to see great distances is that the sky must fill most of the view and this particular panorama was a first-class meteorological laboratory. It was open to the sea and felt the full force of the prevailing westerly winds as depression followed depression and cold front followed warm front for year after year. My classroom was the ideal observation post and while this weather contributed to my lively interest in geography, it did nothing to improve my love of athletics.

I was not particularly gifted at my studies or sport, but whereas the former responded to hard work, the latter remained obdurate. I thought it was so unfair that the more I trained at hurdling and javelin throwing the more tense and less successful I became. Even the weather mocked my efforts as the running track and the javelin throwing area both faced the west wind, and the heavy rainfall made the ground too soft for sprinting. Along the school hedge were a number of stunted oak trees whose bare trunks rose about ten feet from the ground before giving up the struggle with the wind and trailing off to the east in long leafless fingers. These gaunt monuments were constant reminders of the hopelessness of trying to compete with the wind and rain as well as my competi-

tors and myself. How sensible it would be to play a sport which made use of the elements, which called for no natural ability and which gave some reward for hard work.

When I was seventeen I managed to cajole my father into replacing the black bicycle with a lightweight racing machine. It was red with drop handlebars, derailleur gears and cable brakes which combined with my greater strength made excursions to the sheltered south coast easier than hitherto. I had visited the Fal river a few times with my parents and it had made a deep impression on me. It richly deserves the praise of the Memoirs of the Geological Survey which unashamedly labels it the most beautiful inland waterway in England. It is hard to believe that this peaceful and sheltered ria is such a short distance from the baleful north coast. The Fal river and Carrick Roads empty into Falmouth Bay, which in turn is sheltered from the open Atlantic by the Lizard peninsula. Only a southerly gale seriously disturbs the peace of the river and this pales into insignificance beside the furies which break on the north coast in winter. The Fal is not really a river in the accepted sense but is an old river valley which has fallen below sea level to become a flooded arm of the sea. Its banks are well wooded, it abounds in small creeks and quiet anchorages, and I spent much of my spare time exploring its scenery along the shore and its history in the local library. I was enchanted by a small forgotten quay at Greatwood. There are several large houses along the Fal; in the past each one had its own slate quay at which the stone for building the house was unloaded and, later, coal was delivered. They have all fallen into disuse and the quay at Greatwood can only be reached by an overgrown path through the woods. This was a place to dream of the future, and I returned time and again to lie hidden in the deep grass and watch the slow events of the river by poking a pair of binoculars through the high stalks. The quay overlooks the entrance to Mylor creek, the yacht

5

harbour, Mylor Pool, and across the Carrick Roads to St. Just in Roseland. It was my special delight to watch the yachts swinging quietly at their moorings in summer and to follow the oyster dredging boats in winter. How beautiful the yachts seemed, how little used they were, how they synthesised my yearnings to use the weather instead of fighting against it. On this quay the thought came that a yacht such as one of these could carry me to the most distant of the countries that so absorbed my interest in geography books. At Greatwood I decided to sail to the Caribbean to do geographical research.

I first went sailing when I was nineteen. The family doctor took me out for an afternoon in his small cruising boat and I remember plying him with questions about the merits and costs of the boats that we passed. For two years I had been buying all the sailing magazines that my pocket money could buy. I had been given the books that Eric Hiscock had written about cruising, and these I duly read from cover to cover and have used for reference ever since. By reading, imagining and by watching the boats from the shore I had anticipated exactly what it would be like to sail, and my reaction to this first cruise was that I had done it all before. A week later I flew to the U.S.A. and spent three and a half months working my way round the States, Canada and Mexico. Two weeks' work as a gardener in Berkeley, California, gave me enough money for twelve weeks' travelling. This trip convinced me that journeying with a notebook and sailing were different forms of practical geography and that my interest in both sprang from a common source. Equally, I saw that the high wages in the United States would help me to save for the vessel I had set my heart on in no more than two years. That autumn I went up to St. Edmund Hall, Oxford, to read geography and the following summer I went as surveyor and geographer on the Oxford University Expedition to Northern Persia. It was then that I realized that travelling in company is not necessarily the happiest form of expedition. This discovery hardened my early ambition to cruise singlehanded, but sharpened my awareness of the fact that this solution was borne of weakness not strength. Conversely, such a cruise might prove to be a catharsis and general putting in order of my own house so that I might gain a justifiable confidence in dealing with other people.

In 1964 I was due to lead an Oxford University expedition to Guatemala but this fell through because we found it practically impossible to get visas for a group survey. Perhaps it was just as well, because the summer of 1964 found me confined to the Radcliffe Hospital recovering from the amoebic dysentery that I had caught in Persia. In hospital I was not allowed to move, and during the long hours spent in bed I decided to return to America and save enough money for my West Indies expedition. Four weeks later I went sailing for the second time. For the remainder of that summer and for all of the following season I crewed in a West of England Redwing. There was a small and dwindling class of these splendid 14-foot dinghies at the Restronguet Sailing Club and we raced them on my beloved Carrick Roads. For me, dinghy sailing was strictly an apprenticeship for the larger offshore yachts, and I often wondered how many dinghy sailors used their boats as Walter Mitty-type props for offshore sailing.

I took a second class honours degree at Oxford and in September 1965 I returned to New York as master in charge of geography at St. Bernard's School. Towards the end of the month I chartered a yacht in the Virgin Islands for a spring vacation sail training venture. During the term before the cruise I taught the boys the rudiments of sailing with the help of model yachts on the pond in Central Park. They visited the Planetarium; they were taught drown-proofing and simple navigation. The highlight of the term was a film which showed Sir Thomas Lipton's repeated attempts to win the America's Cup. The boys at the school had little opportunity to lead a typical boy's life in a city as violent and dangerous as New York, and since they were a little young for sail training I was both delighted and amazed at the way they responded. Two masters and six boys on a 40-foot boat in the trade winds was an ideal environment in which they could spread their wings.

Life aboard a sailing vessel demands a measure of self-discipline and group discipline that is impossible to emulate in the classroom. The leaders and the led emerged very quickly, but this hierarchy was thrown into confusion by switching the order of the watches. A small vessel with a simple rig meant that the crew spent the minimum length of time getting orientated to the boat, and after three or four days they could be put in charge of a watch while I pretended to sleep. The change in confidence and manner when the boys returned to school was most marked and in several cases their interest in their studies improved.

In the summer of 1966 I returned to Cornwall and spent much of my time racing a 10-ton sloop around the buoys and on short passage races up and down the coast. My first year's savings had come up to expectations, but after analysing the second-hand boat market it was obvious that I would have to double my earnings during the following academic year in order to purchase my boat the next summer. The owner of the boat that I had chartered in the Caribbean offered me an evening job in his placement agency, so I had to forfeit my leisure activity of preparing a new geography textbook. His Madison Avenue office worked two shifts a day and was solely concerned with moving highly paid executives from one job to another and taking 10 per cent of their first year's salary en route.

The records of the agency's clients were stored in the memory bank of a computer. When a vacancy occurred its details were fed into the computer which then supplied the names of a dozen or more suitable applicants. I was very excited by the competitiveness of the organization and the originality of its president. I was unwilling to return to the slothful pace of the New York Central Library which had been my second home during my first year in New York and I became increasingly uneasy about my plans to do a Ph.D. degree in the West Indies. Was a Ph.D. of real value for the sort of work I intended to do? Was I using the research as an excuse to sail? Was I still interested in cruising or had the frenetic pace and ambitious atmosphere of Madison Avenue converted me into a racing sailor?

During Thanksgiving I had three days' holiday and took Eric Tabarly's book *Lonely Victory* to the country with me. This described his win in the second singlehanded Transatlantic Race in 1964.

The first race had been held in 1960 and the idea was the brainchild of Colonel H. G. Hasler. As a marine commando during the war Hasler had led some canoes up the Garonne River to Bordeaux and had sunk several ships with limpet mines, and many people considered that the idea of a solo race east to west across the Atlantic was only a little less hazardous than Hasler's wartime adventure. There had been some solo racing during the last century, but this event in 1960 was the first yacht race of any kind in this direction across the Western Ocean. The race was sponsored by *The Observer* newspaper and organised by the Royal Western Yacht Club at Plymouth. The five competitors prepared their boats well, although the techniques of singlehanded sailing were less well known then than now. Francis Chichester won this race from Plymouth to the Ambrose Light Vessel near New York in forty days, eleven hours. He sailed *Gipsy Moth III*, a 40-foot sloop which had been designed by Robert Clark.

Two years later Chichester sailed across the Atlantic alone in an attempt to beat his previous time. *Gipsy Moth III* was now rigged as a cutter and Chichester sent daily radio messages to *The Guardian*. His new record of thirty-three and a half days made him the favourite for the second singlehanded Transatlantic Race in 1964 when the finish of the race was changed to Newport, Rhode Island. Although Chichester bettered his personal target of thirty days he was beaten by a comparatively unknown Frenchman, Lieutenant Eric Tabarly. When Robert Clark designed *Gipsy Moth III* in 1958 he did not know that it would be entered in a singlehanded race and so Chichester was at a disadvantage in competing against Tabarly's 44-foot ketch which had been built with the sole intention of winning the 1964 race.

I was impressed with Tabarly's attitude to the event. It was clear that he had driven the boat in the same 'devil-take-the-hindmost' attitude that is more commonly associated with offshore racing in crewed yachts. He did not regard the crossing as a long and arduous cruise, but he had a fiercely competitive outlook which helped him to keep the boat going fast even when his self-steering broke down after only eleven days at sea. The layout and design of the boat, his sleeping habits and his constant sail changing all reflected his determination to win the race. Whereas most of the competitors in both 1960 and 1964 had come to the race with a cruising background and a cruising attitude, Tabarly had done a considerable amount of racing with the Royal Ocean Racing Club.

During that autumn I was teaching by day and working in the agency by night. I had averaged four and a half hours sleep per day for four months. More than once I had worked right through the night, starting school without even a break for breakfast. New York brought out the competitive spirit in me, and my way of life at that time made me very sympathetic to the manner in which Tabarly won the race. I was sure that my outlook had changed, and in the grime, the traffic congestion and the concrete chasms of New York I came to know that I no longer wanted to go cruising—now I wanted to race my boat! Equally, the single-handed Transatlantic Race seemed a much more direct and honest way of working out my bizarre emotions than my devious designs on the Caribbean!

The construction of Tabarly's *Pen Duick III* seemed very simple and I thought this must have been a cheap boat to build. I wondered if I could build a similar, though larger, yacht for the 1968 singlehanded Transatlantic Race, so I busied myself by writing to six British yacht designers saying that I had saved three thousand pounds and was there any chance of my building a boat that could win the 1968 race?

While sailing at Mylor I was particularly impressed by a boat called *Joliette* that had been designed by Robert Clark in 1950. It was very well sailed by George Corke who readily sang the praises of the boat's architect and added that all of Clark's boats had the reputation of being easy and steady on the helm. After experimenting with a Hasler steering gear in the Caribbean I could see that this feature would be of great value for a single-handed yacht. As luck would have it Robert Clark's was the only letter that gave me any hope of fulfilling my dream. He said that he did not know how much such a boat would cost but that I should consider the possibility of commercial sponsorship. I was not sure what this implied although the example of our sponsored expedition to Northern Persia was clear in my mind. I replied that I thought it would be very difficult to convince a sponsor of my ability as I was only twenty-four years old and had done very little sailing. I outlined what experience I had, said that I was confident that I could do the job if given the right tool, and if he still felt I could raise the necessary sponsorship then I would fly home to discuss it with him.

I was very anxious because it was already December 1966 and I was worried lest it might be too late to get such a weighty project off the ground, but Clark replied by return, 'Fly home immediately.' This threw me into a quandary since the added expense of going home for Christmas would seriously erode my savings for doing a Ph.D. in the Caribbean and give me little hope of going back to these plans if sponsorship was not forthcoming. Secondly, I was very unhappy about the thought of sponsorship attracting publicity and advertising. My reasons for entering the race were personal and introverted and I wanted to leave Plymouth unseen sailing an unknown boat without any sponsored ballyhoo. With my limited experience the ballyhoo could only be an embarrassment to my sponsors. I disliked advertising and the flavour of publicity that surrounded non-events.

I carried Clark's letter in my breast pocket for five days, rereading his well-phrased paragraphs hundreds of times. I analysed every sentence and tried to elaborate on his concise ideas. Eventually I quashed my prissy, puritan morals about sponsorship with the argument that I was unlikely to win the race without some financial help, and since I did not know what was involved in sponsorship it was pointless to start worrying about it at this stage.

Having settled this worry I started to have sleepless nights tossing and turning as I battled with the most ferocious storms imaginable. A vivid imagination inhibits action. Every night for a week I was regularly clawing my way off the lee shore of the North Cliffs in a full gale and being washed off the foredeck mere seconds before waking up. The worst nightmare of all was seeing a girl-friend moving like a wraith along a beach at Newport and waving a silk shawl in the wind. No matter how hard I tried, it was impossible for me to sail my boat towards Newport. The boat seemed incapable of pointing any closer than ninety-degrees to the west winds while this beautiful girl bewitched the vessel.

I was destined in my dreams to reach up and down the Atlantic forever without getting nearer the finish of the race. Eventually, after competing in the race well over a hundred times and surviving the most appalling catastrophes, I plucked up enough courage to cable Clark: 'Flying home, arrive Heathrow 10.40., 19th December.'

2

The Sponsorship Trail

It was with considerable trepidation that I walked along Piccadilly to Robert Clark's office. For six years I had been planning a cruise to the West Indies and here I was burning my savings on what might well turn out to be a wild-goose chase. To stand a chance of doing well in the 1968 singlehanded Transatlantic Race I would have to build a boat as large as those of my competitors. This is because a boat's speed is the square root of its waterline length multiplied by a factor which can vary from .9 to 1.6 to take into account a number of variables such as displacement, hull shape, sail area, type of rig, etc. Therefore, the larger the boat, the faster it will go, the more difficult it will be to handle and the more it will cost.

From what I know now I am convinced that for the foreseeable future the upper limit on the size of the vessel that one man can handle will be imposed by cost rather than difficulties in handling the boat. We did not know this in 1966, and the size of Chichester's *Gipsy Moth IV* which was then circling the world and Tabarly's new *Pen Duick III* made it certain that I would need a boat about 60-foot length overall in order to compete with some hope of success. It was equally certain that my limited funds would not buy the masts and sails for such a boat, and to compete in a yacht that I could afford to build myself would mean that I did not have any hope of winning. And New York had made me sufficiently competitive to want to win very much indeed.

Clark did everything possible to confirm my worst fears. After cordial introductions he firmly announced that he could not help me with sponsorship. Perhaps he thought that I expected him to help with the cost of the boat and I hoped that I did not look that naïve. The main reason for flying home had been to hear Clark expand on the point in his letter '. . . but you should consider commercial sponsorship', and I was aghast to find that sponsorship was not for discussion. It must have been five minutes before I was listening to him again. In my letter I had enquired about a plywood hull and he had prepared some sketches of a double chine vessel about 41-foot length overall. This was the boat that I intended to build myself with my own savings.

Clark made it clear that a sponsored boat would be quite different. My appetite was whetted and I wondered what he was dreaming up, but since the subject of sponsorship was not for discussion, I secretly argued that to ask questions about a budget-free vessel would also be vetoed. I kept quiet. I was put in my place about light displacement. It was discovered that my notions on displacement were pre-Archimedean. It was further discovered that I had never sailed at night, never been to sea alone and, with the exception of two weeks in the Caribbean, my experience of ocean-going yachts was limited to about half a dozen short races. Curiously, Clark seemed rather heartened by these admissions. My pleading guilty to total ignorance of celestial navigation and only a theoretical knowledge of coastal navigation brought such loud laughs that it made his trousers drop a couple of inches off his hips. As he hitched them up he half turned to the window and a normally white face was browned by the December sun to show me what he looked like as a young man. I remember liking what I saw and I warmed to him before lunch with the generous aid of a bottle of Blanc de Blanc that we drank from pewter mugs.

Lunch itself at Clark's club was less than enjoyable. Clark

insisted on pushing me into verbal corners just to see how I would fare. Four months of nineteen hours' work per day topped up by two sleepless nights had taken their toll of any wit that I may have had before and I fared badly. Teatime followed lunch with no perceptible pause. It was extremely difficult to concentrate on details of length, draft, displacement and sail area when it was perfectly obvious that I hadn't enough money even to contemplate these as being practical rather than theoretical questions.

Much later, when teatime was in danger of becoming dinner, a man walked casually from the snooker room. Clark leant across the table with the tone and air of a man asking a great favour. 'Oh, by the way,' he whispered, 'that chap is in advertising. Don't you need a sponsor? Would you like me to broach it with him?' Before replying I waited a few extra micro-seconds in an effort to give my 'yes' a hint of casualness. The topic was raised and immediately shot down in flames. 'All been done before ole boy, not a chance. Here, I've just had a jolly good game of snooker with ole. . . .' His words trailed off into irrelevancies as I retreated into a mental cave to lick my wounds. But I was not to know that the advertising man's presence was something less than accidental or that his parting remark several eons later, 'Here's my card, write and tell me all about it,' would ever lead anywhere. Late that night I wrote to the siren of Newport beach to tell her that everything seemed impossible and that I had been a mug.

Discussion with a naval architect about a boat we both knew was not the vessel for the job but which I could possibly afford and about another boat we both wanted to build but couldn't, is likely to be rather fruitless. Next morning's talk with Clark was just that. Overnight I drove down to Cornwall and arrived in the depths of depression and as white as a sheet. Father and stepmother were pleased to see their son, but were not pleased with the reason for his unexpected Christmas visit. Father, quite rightly, regarded my Transatlantic Race ambitions as being suicidal, but he was not really worried because he was sure that I'd never raise the money. The fact that I could even *entertain* such thoughts was much more disturbing. As I was going to be frustrated in this venture what other terrible target would I set my sights on?

Christmas 1966 was continually punctuated by what appeared to be my family's favourite phrase 'lack of experience'. My retort, that one only gets experience by doing things that one has not done before, did nothing to ease their minds. 'Surely experience is directly related to intelligence,' I argued. 'The more intelligent one is, the less one has to be shown how to deal with every situation and the more one can extrapolate from a limited first hand knowledge.' I thought that I had done enough sailing to know what was likely to be involved in crossing the Atlantic alone and to bring into perspective all the reading that I intended to do on my rather special subject. I had only steered a boat for about ten hours but concluded that if my self-steering arrangements were sufficiently sound then I might well do no more steering than this during the entire race. On the other hand I had done a fair amount of crewing and had made a study of self-steering gears, and this would prove more important than my incompetence as a helmsman. As a professional geographer I was not unduly worried about my ignorance of navigation, and since I intended to build the boat myself I thought it unlikely that I would be embarrassed by any gear failures. The fact that I had not completed a successful mortice and tenon joint in woodwork classes at school was quite beside the point! If I completed the boat the chances were that it would be sound. So little was known about singlehanded sailing that a fresh brain on the subject stood as much chance of success as one that was fettered by convention. And in any case I had eighteen months in which to prepare. If preparations went according to plan then I should be ready to sail in June 1968, but if preparations went their own way then 1969 would be a better year for me.

Soon after getting home I was scouring my favourite stretch of water—Carrick Roads. At Mylor I bumped into Bill Jennings and Paul Williams with whom I had been sailing the previous summer. In an off hand sort of way I let slip that I was interested in the singlehanded race in 1968. To my surprise and to their eternal credit they gave me every encouragment and help.

I had read about Derek Kelsall's method of building *Toria*. This was the trimaran in which he had won the Round Britain Race earlier that year. He was building trimarans and catamarans at Wadebridge, and on Boxing Day I drove over to see him. The method consisted of laying up glass reinforced plastic on either side of a non-porous foam called Plasticell. The sandwich or foam core method seemed to have a number of advantages over ply-wood. It was a monocoque type of construction with no seams or joints; the designer was not restricted to the hard chine shape; it was lighter and promised to be both easier to build and cheaper. I bounced up and down on some spare sections of a trimaran hull and they seemed impressively strong. However, the square panels of foam did not take up the compound curve of the mould and this gave the hull a series of flats along its length. Although the actual surface was smooth I was very worried about the unfair-ness of the overall shape.

Kelsall assured me that the solution to this problem was merely a matter of hard work, and despite the fact that he had not built a keel yacht by this method, he was confident that all the difficulties could be overcome. I reported all this to Clark and was surprised to get a letter by return saying that he had designed a run of twenty such boats that had been built in Italy some years before. The foam core method was not new and had been tried with varying success in the United States, Holland and France. The main difficulty had been in finding a suitable core material, and

1. Immediately *Lipton* felt well balanced and my hopes for the race soared.

2. The keel pattern.

Plasticell, which B.T.R. Industries were manufacturing under licence from Goodrich, seemed to be the answer.

I sent a letter to the advertising man and had a long and helpful discussion with him when I returned to London. He outlined what he thought sponsors might require, suggested ways in which I might present my case and brought the whole question of sponsorship into perspective. This, too, was reported to Clark, who replied, saying that he was convinced that a sponsor could be secured, but it was my job to seek one out. I was encouraged, but not convinced, and flew back to New York bubbling with ideas. For the next eighteen months, as I ate, slept, worked and played, the race was continually on my mind.

The problem seemed to break itself down into five parts— sponsorship, design, building, navigation and psychology. In many ways the last factor seemed the most important of all. Clark and I discussed this aspect of the race as much as any other. To drive a boat at its fastest when one is alone one must be happy, and a number of decisions about the boat and build-up for the race were tested with the question, 'When I am cold, wet, seasick, frightened, tired and want to go home will this make things better or worse?'

Before I could become an adequate foil for Clark I would have to study my subject more thoroughly. In New York Central Library I read all the post-war books on design, ocean racing, cruising and boatbuilding. Until this time I had never looked at a vessel's hull shape with any understanding of how variations between two boats might affect their relative performance. Books on yacht design left me bewildered until I studied *Model Racing Yachts* by Priest and Lewis. I was able to watch yachts similar to the ones they described sailing every weekend on the pond in Central Park. I spent hours watching their performance and then studying their shapes in the boathouse. Model yachts were particularly relevant to my case because they were steered by very sophisticated self-steering units. After my study in miniature I was able to go back to the more advanced works on yacht design with fresh understanding. The best way to appreciate the enormity of a yacht designer's task and the brilliance of a really successful design is to draw up one's own boats on a drawing-table. I used an extra large drawing-board borrowed from the school art room, bought splines, pigs, curves, paper and a planimeter and set to work on a series of hideously unsuccessful designs.

I plied boat builders with questions about their methods and studied the technical data issued by the manufacturers of glass-fibre and combed back numbers of sailing magazines so that I could build up a comprehensive picture of the techniques used for building glassfibre boats in American yards. The four builders using the foam core method must have been very irritated by my persistent interrogation. Within six months my files of notes and cuttings weighed over fifty pounds and I had collected two trunk loads of books. The writings of Chichester, Hasler and Tabarly came in for close scrutiny as did the pilot charts of the North Atlantic.

In the spring of 1967 I started to get fit for the race. This was not at all popular with the boys at the school as it meant that on four afternoons a week in all weathers and with the temperature often below freezing they were chased over the rough ground of Central Park for ever-increasing distances and at ever-increasing speeds. But at least the boys were spared the cold showers which I hoped would improve my resistance to the low temperatures of the mid-Atlantic in June.

All these preparations looked like going off with the excitement of a damp squib as that rare animal, the commercial sponsor, seemed so elusive that I almost gave him up for extinct. I anticipated that companies might worry about backing such a traditional sport as yachting, so I wrote to the President of the Royal Yachting Association to ask his opinion. Prince Philip's equerry said that he approved of sponsorship as long as the advertising was in good taste, and I quoted his statement in my letters. During the first half of 1967 I wrote over three thousand letters and spent two hundred and seventy pounds in an effort to extend my proposed boat from forty-four feet to sixty-one feet overall. Robert had drawn up a medium displacement yawl and I sent the profile and general arrangement drawings to the chairmen of hundreds of British companies. I was not keen to get American backing although this might have been more forthcoming. We expected the yawl to cost £30,000 and I outlined details of the method of building, the estimate, the timetable, and the vessel's characteristics. The prodigious quantity of mail that found its way into my pigeon-hole each day and the surreptitious way in which I collected it between lessons was a constant source of amusement to the school secretary. I was told 'No' in a thousand different and often charming ways.

Ian Brett, who worked in the trade section of the British Consulate in New York, was very original and helpful with suggestions about possible sponsors. One of Ian's suggestions was that I should get a computer to do all my navigation. I couldn't quite see the point of that, but it started me wondering if a computer could help me with the daily course planning relative to the forecasted weather. I wrote to English Electric Computers and asked them if they could help. At the same time I sent off another batch of over one hundred and fifty letters asking for sponsorship. These letters were posted just before I went to the Virgin Islands with a party of boys for a second sail-training cruise. Three weeks later I returned to yet another mountain of 'Noes' and a solitary 'Yes'. English Electric would consider my proposal in detail when I was next in England. It now seemed probable that I would have the benefit of computerised course predictions without having a boat fast enough to take advantage of them.

For six months I had heard from Clark about twice a week and my letters had changed slowly from 'Dear Mr. Clark', to 'Dear Clark' to 'Dear Robert' as he continued to give good advice and much needed encouragement. We agreed that while Sir Francis Chichester's voyage established a useful precedent, most companies would want to see him safe in England before putting money into another singlehanded venture. I gave up my job at St. Bernard's and flew home in early June. Robert and I had a long council of war to try to decide why I had not managed to raise any sponsorship when a number of other people had. We came to the conclusion that it was too much to expect one sponsor to cover the entire cost of the 61-foot yawl and we had better reduce the size of the boat and try to get items of boat equipment sponsored separately. If the additional capital could not be found within a month then I should go ahead with my smaller boat.

Already it was very late and I wanted to be ready for sea trials before the end of February, so the building of a new boat would have to be started in September. The lines and construction drawings would take at least six weeks to prepare so mid-July became the latest possible date before deciding definitely on which boat to build. I alternated between being very depressed and very angry at not being able to go ahead with the larger boat since Robert and I seemed to have laid a sound foundation with our preparations over the previous six months. I sent out the final batch of letters in early July and added one more as an afterthought. This was absolutely the last letter that I intended to write and was prompted by an old advertisement for Lipton's Tea. I wondered why I had not thought of this company before, especially since I had shown the American schoolboys a film of Sir Thomas

Lipton's life. It showed how at the age of fifteen Lipton left Glasgow and worked his passage to New York. He spent four years in America before returning to Scotland and setting up a grocer's shop. He was one of the first retailers to appreciate the value of advertising, and within fifteen years he had set up a chain of stores.

Lipton was already a millionaire when he visited Colombo and bought up a number of tea plantations which started the tea-blending business for which he is better remembered today. It was in 1898 that he first challenged for the America's Cup in his yacht *Shamrock* and there followed four more unsuccessful attempts to win the Cup. I found that Lipton (Retail) Ltd. and Lipton Overseas were part of Allied Suppliers, and Lipton Inc., the successor to the American side of the business, was now part of Unilever. Lipton (Retail) Ltd. administered the chain of grocery shops and supermarkets in this country while Lipton Overseas was concerned with the tea market. I addressed my letter to Mr. Malcolm Cooper, the Chairman of Allied Suppliers, and he replied to say that the proposal would be brought forward for further discussions in a week's time. This had happened a number of times before and was not a signal for premature optimism. In the meantime I had asked Robert to go ahead with the lines of a 44-foot cutter, but we were both acutely aware that this solution was only a stopgap.

A week later Mr. Cooper telephoned to say that the board had agreed to sponsor the proposed vessel as long as the cost did not rise above the figure I had quoted. I gave a whoop of delight and went racing along to Robert's office to find that he had gone to Holland to see his draughtsman. His secretary eventually traced him by telephone and I told him to hold his horses on the 44-foot cutter as we had enough money to extend it to a 53-foot ketch. The boat's name *Sir Thomas Lipton* would be a throwback to the sixteenth century when all sailing vessels were masculine. At last we were 'in business. During the summer I wrote to all the manufacturers of yacht equipment and the industrial firms which would supply the resin, glassfibre and Plasticell for the hull, and they were all very generous in giving sizeable discounts or free issues.

Just before leaving New York I had broken my arm playing Rugby and my first sail was not until the R.O.R.C. race to Duarnenez. Paul Williams and I sailed in Bill Jennings's boat *Tilly Witch*, and the second day of the race we met a severe gale with winds up to Force 10. We ran for twelve hours from Ushant to the Lizard with steep and regular seas rising alarmingly in our wake. I had practically no sleep for four days and my navigation and lack of seasickness gave me great confidence for the following year.

Robert Clark and I were the guests of Commander David Seth-Smith on *Griffin III* during a Cowes week which was dominated by *Pen Duick III*, Eric Tabarly's brilliant wishbone schooner. I watched her crew of nine all working like demons and wondered how he intended to sail that complicated boat alone.

I met Les Williams and he thought that Tabarly had seen the futility of trying to point high into the wind in the Atlantic and had built a schooner with the idea of driving fast on a close reach. I was not convinced that he was right and in the draft of an article for *The Daily Telegraph* I asked if Tabarly was going to repeat what he did in 1964 and scrap his first boat to build another.

For the Fastnet Race I filled a vacancy on *Roundabout*, and it was revealing to see how hard she was driven by her skipper, Johnny Coote. We finished fourth in our class and reached Millbay dock in mid-afternoon where I was delighted to find Father waiting for me. He had been very surprised when I told him that I was being sponsored and began to change his ideas about my competing in the race. Meeting me at the end of the Fastnet was a sure signal of his support which was to prove so comforting during the coming year.

3

The Thinking behind
Sir Thomas Lipton

When Robert Clark was twenty-five years old his left eye was removed to relieve the congestion of his sinus. He was in hospital for some weeks, and while his eyes were bandaged he thought up the lines of his first boat. It was built by a friend and turned out to be a great success. Appropriately, it carried the name of *Mystery* and was the forerunner of a class of twelve similar vessels.

Three recent designs by Robert show a great range of imagination. There is *Longbow*, with its scimitar shape profile and full stern. She distinguished herself in 1968 by winning more points in the R.O.R.C. championship than any other boat. *Sea Spirit* is a 50-ton ketch built in steel to be used for sail training at Gordonstoun School and an 80-ton schooner recently completed in Hong Kong is designed as an ocean-going home. Earlier boats include *Caprice of Huon*, designed in 1950 but which swept the board at Cowes Week as recently as 1965, and a three-masted schooner *Carita*, which is one of the world's largest sailing vessels. Despite the different roles for which these boats have been designed, they all have an unmistakable air which brings an 'Ah, that's a Clark boat' from the pundits.

For Robert there is none of the endless trial and error with pencil and rubber. While walking through the park or sitting in his chair when other people have gone to bed he will be thinking about a new commission. He has waited as long as three months before he has been happy with a new yacht, and only when his mind's eye can see the boat sailing is he ready to set out the main characteristics from which his draughtsman will complete the drawings.

I can trace the four leaps that have established the way in which I think. At my primary school, arithmetic was a kind of mechanical game in which numbers did things to one another in a variety of unexpected ways and the result was extremely difficult to forecast with any confidence. Later, a master took me aside and carefully explained that if I used some *common sense* in checking my work it would become quite obvious that my more original answers were preposterous. At my secondary school, I learnt that a strong *interest* in what one is doing can generate ability. At Oxford I learnt how to *synthesise* my thoughts, but I had to wait until I met Robert to appreciate the art of *analysis*.

After the leading dimensions of the vessel and the overall policy for its design had been decided in the secret of Robert's mind, he was kind enough to settle the details in open debate. We spent well over fifty hours analysing the problems and recording the answers in a big notebook.

The size of a singlehander's boat is limited by the sails he can handle; so we started with the rig. Its type was influenced by my lack of experience, the weather conditions for the North Atlantic in June and our ambition to have a rig which would help the boat to steer itself. In trying to anticipate the weather I would meet, Robert's experience in crossing the Atlantic from west to east in *Joliette* proved invaluable. I studied the pilot charts which show average conditions over the past thirty-five years and visited the Meteorological Office to see actual weather maps of previous Junes.

In an average June I could expect a high percentage of moderate to strong head winds in mid-Atlantic while on the Grand Banks and close to the American shore the wind would probably be

SIR THOMAS LIPTON

Length overall	56·16′ (17·1m.) (57′ with bumpkin)	Length waterline:	42′ (12·83 m.)
Beam	12′ (3·65m.)	Draft	8′ (2·44m.)
Displacement	12·25 tons	Sail Area	1171 sq. ft. (109 sq. m.)
Ballast	7·25 tons	Mainsail	408 (39 sq. m.)
		Trysail	280 (26 sq. m.)
		No. 1 jib	703 (67·8 sq. m.)
Ballast ratio	59%	No. 2 jib	405 (37·7 sq. m.)
		No. 3 jib	214 (19·5 sq. m.)
Rating: R.O.R.C.	41·72′	Ghoster	1020 (95·0 sq. m.)
		Boomed foresail	208 (19·4 sq. m.)
T.C.F.	0·9459	Storm foresail	127 (11·8 sq. m.)
		Mizzen	150 (13·9 sq. m.)
B.S.F.	643·7 s.p.m.	Running sail	630 ea. (58·5 sq. m.)
		Mizzen staysail	420 (39·2 sq. m.)

Owner: Geoffrey J. Williams. *Designer*: Robert Clark. *Builders*: Derek Kelsall and
Geoffrey Williams.

0 2 4 6 8 10
FEET

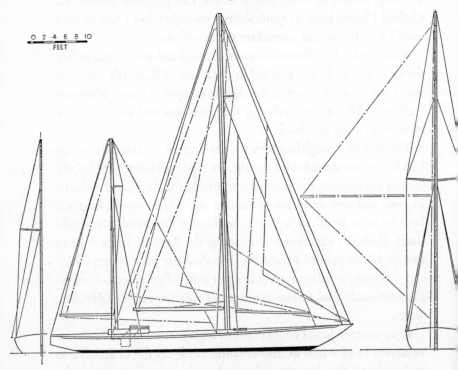

1. *Sir Thomas Lipton*: Sail plan.

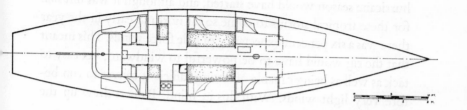

2. *Sir Thomas Lipton:* Arrangement

2. The simple purpose during the race was to win and I wanted this to be reflected in the spirit of my living quarters. There was no concession to unnecessary comfort below decks and I hoped this would give me no excuse to relax my efforts. Standing headroom, a W.C., a wash basin and hanging lockers were all strangers to the ship and I very much regretted the cuckoo-like intrusion of the generating plant, electrics and the radio-telephone. These were only tolerated because they helped me to keep in touch with the world. The generating plant was just aft of the main mast, together with a large bank of batteries. The very large chart table on the port side, with shelves and lockers around, provided the navigating and radio department; with the galley opposite. Having a settee on either side amidships I could always sit on the comfortable side. I did not need the ten berths that were fitted in addition, but it was convenient to have a choice of two of them, and the other eight were in effect all stowage bins. I could only stand up under the small coachroof next forward of the small cockpit, but I had so much useful space, and it was so simply arranged, that I could live well and things never got in a muddle.

29

light and variable. If, as was possible, a zone of high pressure sat across my track for an extended period then this could mean very light winds in mid-Atlantic. Beam winds were likely to be of short duration but it was possible that I would get light to moderate easterly winds during the first thousand miles. The hurricane season would have started, and although it was unusual for these tropical storms to come so far north so early in the year there was a six per cent expectancy of gale force winds. This meant that the rig would have to be powerful to windward, yet easy to tack as well as being capable of setting sufficient canvas to run before very light winds. With this in mind, Robert drew up the sail plan shown in Fig. 1.

The jib and a mainsail are the principal driving sails, while the boomed foresail and mizzen are steering sails. I was alarmed at sacrificing so much area in the lower foretriangle, and I was afraid that a boomed sail would not set as well, or drive as hard as a low-cut genoa staysail.

Robert made me agree that the yacht with the fastest potential speed was not necessarily going to be the winner, and went on to say that if the boat should happen to come up into the wind and a genoa staysail backed, then in all probability the boat would be thrown on to the other tack. Nothing could be more injurious to a singlehander's speed and morale than a boat that continually put itself about. If a boat with a boomed foresail came up into the wind then the boom would rise and start to move across towards the windward side but the sail would not back and force the boat through the eye of the wind. Furthermore, if the boomed foresail was deliberately sheeted in hard and the mizzen was set free, then when the boat came up into the wind the mizzen would start to back while the foresail was still trying to push the boat off the wind. The reverse would happen if the boat tried to steer away from the wind. This couple would act as a self-steering device to reduce the load on my self-steering gear and to supplement it in an emergency.

We decided to do away with reefing for the mainsail and rely on dropping it on deck and running up a 280 sq. ft. trysail on a separate track. There was an unexpected bonus with this method because as the main boom gooseneck dropped a few inches down the mast, the end of the boom was held inboard by the mizzen forestays which meant that the whole sail dropped on to the deck. Therefore, we ended up with the unusual sight of a boat with a non-reefing mainsail and a roller-reefing mizzen. Reefing the mizzen was a way of reducing the amount of weather helm and another means of trimming the self-steering.

Spinnakers were out of the question. Instead, Robert arranged twin running sails. He argued that it was quite wrong to trap the wind in a V-shape which is what happens when these sails are hanked to the forestay, and it would be much better for the wind to be driven off the sail in the same way that it drives off the working sails. This meant that the stays fell from the mast-head through twin hatches just in front of the mast, and the running sails had a self-steering effect on the boat and could be reefed by allowing their booms to be swept forward in a V-shape.

I followed all of Robert's advice about the rig, but I did not like the conventional hull with the long keel that he drew up in his first proposal. From my talks with Derek Kelsall there seemed no doubt that a canoe-shaped hull with the keel and rudder attached would be easier and cheaper to build than one which incorporated a full reverse turn in the midship section. 'Why can't we have a fin and skeg profile?' I asked. Robert replied that he knew exactly how the conventional boat would feel on the tiller, and since so much depended on the directional stability of the vessel it was far better to stick to something we knew than risk the wild steering qualities common to so many fin and skeg yachts.

The re-emergence of fin and skeg profiles is perhaps the most significant feature of yacht design during the past ten years, and there seems to be no easy way to ensure that a boat will, or will not, be easy to steer. The factors which affect the balance of a boat include the fore and aft shape of the hull, the position of the keel, the position and rake of the mast, the relative sizes of the sails, the position of the sail plan in relation to the profile of the hull, the steepness of the leading edge of the stem and keel and the size of the gap between the fin and the skeg. Robert agreed that there was no reason why a properly designed fin and skeg yacht should not be balanced, but if it was wrong the result was likely to be more alarming than on a full-hulled vessel. The trick lay in getting it right. I added that model yacht designers had more or less abandoned the full keel yacht during the early 1930s and that the latest models were all extreme fin and skeg profiles which balance perfectly well and are steered by sensitive vane gears. Robert was not convinced, but lack of money finally forced his hand.

When he drew up the first proposal we did not have a budget, but when *Sir Thomas Lipton* was in mind we were bound to a certain figure. This meant that we would get a longer, lighter and faster boat for our money if Robert abandoned the full hull shape. This he finally did, and when the lines arrived in August it was exactly what I would have liked to have drawn, had I had the wit. It seemed right from every angle and I was struck by the single-mindedness of its shape. Here was a racing hull designed for speed under sail with no thought for the R.O.R.C. rating rules or accommodation. It had the minimum freeboard necessary to stop water coming over green, and its high ballast ratio and uncluttered decks would give me a clear and stable working platform.

Lipton has no auxiliary engine, no W.C., no wash-basin, no hanging lockers, no standing head-room, and its berths are made up of Pirelli webbing stretched across aluminium tubes. The only concession to opulence below deck is a very large, adjustable chart-table around which are grouped all my navigational instruments and the radio-telephone. Opposite is the galley where I could sit to choose, prepare and eat my food without having to leave my place. By modern standards the accommodation would be classed as spartan, but the design of the entire boat was directed at a particular race, to be sailed by a specific person on a set date, and while this contributed in a real way to the vessel's speed the most important effect was on my attitude.

I was sure that as the race wore on and I became more tired and despondent, there would be a great incentive to drive the boat to the maximum if I knew that I had done nothing which I would ever want to change. Once the rot set in and one began to divide one's purpose, then it would be easy to comfort one's lack of effort by saying, 'Ah well, it will be a grand boat for cruising later on.' Unless I made the best use of him during the 1968 race then I would never have a second chance to justify *Lipton*'s existence.

To my eyes *Sir Thomas Lipton* is a supremely beautiful yacht, and the sail plan and line drawings which are framed on my wall are the two most satisfying illustrations that I have. Robert had designed a boat that seemed right in the beginning and went on to become perfect for me in 1968.

4

Building at Sandwich

I warned Derek Kelsall at the earliest opportunity that I had been sacked from school woodwork classes but he was brave enough to let me work in his yard. In late September Derek moved to the Little Stonar Boatyard near Sandwich, and from then until the end of April I was completely involved in building my new toy. Dozens of lorries delivered hundreds of items to the yard, and it gave me great satisfaction to see Robert's sculpture rise slowly out of barrels of resin and baulks of timber.

I used the lines plan and table of offsets to draw the shape of the hull's cross section on sheets of hardboard. From these we made fifteen frames and set them upside down on the floor of the shed. I had read that Alain Gliksman intended to build a yawl 42.6 feet long on the waterline, and I was worried lest the extra length would make his boat faster than mine. To remedy this we set the frames an extra two inches apart and stretched my waterline length to 42 feet. We fastened battens to the frames and within two weeks of moving into the yard our lath mould, or former, was complete. At the end of the second week we employed young Derek—a fifteen-year-old boy who came to us straight from the local school—and within six weeks the three of us completed Lipton's hull.

The first step involved attaching expanded P.V.C. or Plasticell to the lath mould. Young Derek disappeared inside the mould for hours at a time while we bent the sheets of Plasticell around the

3A. The mould, with sheets of plasticell bent around the curves of the hull.

3B. Derek Kelsall.

4. (*over page*) The mould is broken out in sections. ▷

curves of the hull so that he could fasten them. It was very encouraging to see the shape of the boat emerge so quickly, and we soon laid up three layers of glass fibre on top. The weave of the glass fibre was laid along the water lines, the buttocks and the sections, and a final layer was added around the mast steps and along the keel. A scrim levelled off the pimples in the woven roving, and a month of sanding and filling had to be done before I was satisfied with the fairness of the hull. Derek and I racked our brains for weeks trying to solve this expensive problem, and now that I have been shown the simple answer I am wondering why we were so foolish not to spot it. To ensure that the resin cured properly, all our work had to be done in a dry shed at a temperature of over sixty degrees Fahrenheit.

We had a number of scares which had me running around like a nervous hen. The generating engine often broke down, leaving us with no heat, and twice the Stour broke through the retaining dam and flooded the work area. As we were turning the hull over one of the cables that was holding the boat in position snapped with an impressive twang and let our freshly painted boat slide across the concrete floor and land with all its weight on top of a steel hammer. There was a frightful screeching noise and I expected to see a gaping hole in the topsides but instead we had great difficulty in finding any scratch at all.

The mould was broken out in sections and glass fibre laid up across the beam of the boat. When all the battens had been lifted out, the woven roving was laid along the line of the hull to complete the foam sandwich. Some local welders came in to tailor steel frames to the shape of the hull. They bent a four-inch diameter steampipe along the stem to take the forward chainplates and another pipe ran aft as far as the rudder stock. The frames and gaspipes were bolted to a steel keelplate and all the steelwork was glassed into the hull. The keel would be bolted to the keelplate and this meant that all the major stresses from the rigging to the foot of the keel would be taken by a steel corset. Derek was sure that the steel framing was unnecessary, but it was a good feeling to have this bonus strength.

In late November we heard that Eric Tabarly was going to build a 65-foot trimaran. I was not surprised that he was worried about *Pen Duick III* and her schooner rig, but I did not expect 1967's high priest of yacht racing to change his faith and switch over to the multihull camp. Derek Kelsall and Tabarly had sailed from Wadebridge to Gravesend in the trimaran *Toria* when she was taken to the Boat Show early in the year, and he had been very impressed by the boat's speed off the wind. He must have been strongly influenced by the memory of the race in 1964 when there was a higher percentage of beam winds than are shown on the pilot charts and considerably more than had been experienced by Chichester in 1960 and 1962. Tabarly had started with the best boat for the 1964 race, and I was encouraged to see that although *Pen Duick III* had proved to be a fast boat and would, with re-rigging, be suitable for the race, he was not prepared to mix it with other competitors whose boats were of similar length and speed. Tabarly seemed far from happy with the idea of his new trimaran and remarked, 'It's not a real boat, I just need it to win the race!'

On December 7th I wrote in my diary: 'Surely it is too late to launch such an immense project. The problems of monohulls, their gear and self-steering are comparatively well known, but Tabarly is running into a new field of research, design and development within six months of the toughest race for yachts that has yet been devised. He is taking a real flier, and I think that Les Williams and Alain Gliksman must now rate as more formidable opponents than Tabarly.'

Derek Kelsall's heart is in trimarans and he was delighted that Tabarly had changed his mind. He looked at my boat with renewed interest and mused about his potential as the centre hull for a trimaran.

My training continued throughout the winter. Three or four times a week I went running or did weight training and always followed this with a cold shower. I wore as few clothes as possible and slept with only two blankets on the bed. Whenever a gale was blowing I found it difficult to sleep, and I would toss and turn in my bed trying to imagine what it would be like to sail *Lipton* in those conditions. The only remedy was to get up, put on shorts and a sweater and run along the beach and the pier. After running into the teeth of the gale with the wind tearing at my hair and the rain soaking my body I would feel better and return home exhausted and ready for sleep.

In early January luck, inflamed by my bad management, turned against me and from then until June 1st everything that could go wrong did go wrong. We had fallen behind our schedule and I started to work overtime with two or three of the men. A twelve-hour day became the norm, and without the loyal help of Jim Gilchrist, Derek Champ and Peter Bliss the boat would never have been ready on time. Derek and Jim often worked a seventy-hour week, and it seemed that the total building time would be over five thousand man-hours. This meant that we would start sailing in April instead of February, and we realised that if we found anything seriously wrong with the boat during trials, it would be too late to make changes. One of the main reasons why the fitting out took so long was because the boat was intended for singlehanded sailing. This meant that every item of equipment had to be strengthened or changed in some way. Although most of this equipment was ordered in September some of it did not arrive in time for the race. Resin, glassfibre, Plasticell, yacht instruments and sails were delivered promptly, but all the remaining equipment arrived late. The combination of late delivery and the prototype nature of *Sir Thomas Lipton* resulted in a frightening increase of costs. To the outsider I am sure that it must have appeared that the skippers of sponsored boats had no worries about money. Nothing could be farther from the truth. I sank all my savings in the boat and had borrowed as much as I dared, but I still ran the risk of ending up with a half-finished vessel.

By early February I exhausted my allowance and was desperately worried about the whole project. Liptons had been very generous and the last thing on earth that I wanted was to do an Oliver act. I was about to cancel my order for deck equipment, masts and rigging when the four chairmen of the companies that were sponsoring the boat visited the yard. Bill Jennings had come up from Cornwall and I think they were all surprised at the size of the boat. We had lunch at the Bell Hotel in Sandwich, and after the meal Mr. Malcolm Cooper rose to say that 'they would support the project through to its conclusion'. Bill grabbed my knee under the table and I breathed a huge sigh of grateful relief. I would be able to sleep soundly again that night. A few days later £580 worth of instruments were stolen from the yard. For several weeks there was doubt if they were covered under the terms of the insurance. Although the eighteenth-century language of the policy covered the ship's munitions, arms and grain, it did not seem to account for navigational instruments. This matter was happily resolved only after a long and worrying wait.

Because it was the first sandwich boat to be built in Britain it would have been easy to miscalculate the displacement. To keep a check on this I weighed everything before it was built into the boat, and in February it looked as if we would be floating light. When Robert and I visited the keel makers in east London we decided to remedy this by adding half a ton to the weight of the keel by casting a block of lead into its bottom half. We were

38

hoping that this would bring the boat down to its water-line and improve its stiffness. The wooden keel pattern which was used to shape the hollow in the sand on the foundry floor is made larger than the designed size of the keel to allow for contraction of the molten iron. The amount of contraction varies with each shape, and it is difficult to forecast the final weight with accuracy. We expected our keel to weigh 6.9 tons but it came out to 7.25 tons. If we had left the keel as it was everything would have been all right, but now I was worried about the boat sitting too low in the water. When the keel was delivered we found that the shed was not high enough for the jibs of the cranes to lift the hull on to the keel so we decided to float the completed hull downstream to Richborough Wharf and lift it on to the keel there. The hull slipped into the Stour with impressive speed on March 13th and the workmen—looking like a gang of desperadoes—clambered on board with long bamboo poles to fend the boat off the banks as it moved downstream.

We allowed ourselves ten days to bolt the keel to the hull and fit the skeg into the ventral gap in the counter. The profile of *Sir Thomas Lipton* looks perfect, and at least twice a day I would run back across the fields to gaze at the boat silhouetted against the eastern sky. Passengers in the buses travelling between Sandwich and Ramsgate could be seen staring continuously at this remarkable addition to the landscape. From a distance of a hundred yards it was extremely difficult to judge the length of the boat. It seemed so well proportioned that it could have been 30 feet or 130 feet in length. The visitors and well wishers who had been coming to the yard now poured on to the quay in a never-ending stream, and much time was lost in pleasant chatter. During the last week before the official launching we were working eighteen hours a day, and at the last moment a mistake was made in mixing the resin to seal the gap between hull and keel. I stayed up until 5 a.m.

on the day of the launching trying to fix it, and when we started work again at 6.30 a.m. on March 30th, 1968, it seemed to have set.

A large crowd gathered to see Mr. Snelling name the vessel. He had sailed with Sir Thomas Lipton on the last of the *Shamrocks* and although now 91 he smashed the bottle of champagne over the boat's stem with great gusto. The cranes took a long time to walk the yacht to the edge of the wharf, and when my freshly painted, newly built boat was tottering between the edge of the steel-faced quay and the water, one crane started to topple towards the river. Its back wheels lifted eighteen inches off the concrete and it was saved from capsizing only by the weight of a crowd of people who climbed on to its cabin. The men eased the boat into the water using railway sleepers to fend it clear of the quay. At last it was in the Stour, and Robert and I peered at the waterlines to see how the boat was floating. There was at least two tons of equipment to be added to *Lipton* before he would be ready to leave Plymouth, and we were expecting to see the boat about two inches high. To our horror she was already down on her marks! Robert had designed the freeboard as low as he dared, and losing another two or three inches could be critical.

At this rate it looked as if I would be sailing a submarine and a slow one at that! Robert came on board and we slipped below to have a conference. He opened with the bad news that a strike would delay the standing rigging for another month. I looked down in despair only to be greeted by another horror: water was seeping up through the keel bolts and flooding the bilges! We were late, we were leaking and we were low on our marks. I was depressed beyond belief as I made my way back to the celebration lunch at the Bell Hotel.

That night I spent my first watch on *Lipton* with a gale blowing in from the North Sea. I stayed awake for much of the night pumping out the bilges and tending the mooring lines as the boat rose and fell on the tide. What nonsense! Here I was in the fields of south-east England working like a demon on my boat! What on earth would it be like in the Atlantic?

Next morning Robert cheered me up by remarking that we had launched *Sir Thomas* into fresh water and this would account for his floating lower than designed. It seems that the rising tide does not flow up the river but merely acts as a dam for the fresh-water at the entrance to the Stour. I was not completely con-vinced and risked all kinds of plague during the next few weeks by tasting the river water to test Robert's theory. I survived, Robert was right and *Lipton* was not over-weight. The leaks were more serious, and Derek decided to build pilings on the yard slip-way and bring *Lipton* up on Monday's spring tide. *Lipton* stayed on the slip while a new fairing was glassed in and fitting-out work continued. Two weeks later we assembled to watch the tide lift him out of his berth and we were all nonplussed when the water failed to come within one foot of floating the boat. We could do nothing but wait for the next high tide which was due two weeks later. Last-minute jobs had an unhappy knack of spawning other last-minute jobs, so we were kept very busy during the second fortnight's delay. The depth of water in the Stour is governed by wind direction, the atmospheric pressure and the volume of ground water in addition to the height of the tide. During the last few days, while the moon heaved the tides higher and higher, I walked up and down like an anxious farmer trying to judge when to cut his corn. It would be the final irony to be thwarted at this juncture.

But I need not have worried. At 1.39 a.m., just one minute before the top of the tide, the boat lifted sufficiently for the tractor to pull us clear. Young Derek and Peter came alongside in the tug and we slipped downstream to Richborough under a ghostly moon which lit up the fields and the sea. It took us another week to rig the boat and load all the equipment. At last we were ready, and the problems of actually sailing the boat seemed very small by comparison with all the difficulties of the previous six months.

5A. Praying that it will fit.

5B. (*left to right*): Derek Kelsall, Gardy Barker, the author, Malcolm Cooper and Richard Page.

6A. Sir Thomas Lipton himself.

6B. A large crowd gathered to see Mr. Harold Snelling name the vessel. He sailed with Sir Thomas Lipton on the last of the *Shamrocks* and although now 91 years old he smashed the bottle of champagne over the boat's bow with great gusto.

6C. Robert Clark and the author.

7A. From a distance it was extremely difficult to judge the length of the boat. It seemed so well proportioned that it could have been 30 or 130 feet in length.

7B. The boatbuilders: (*left to right foreground*) Jim Gilchrist, Brian Bootes and Derek Champ.

8. Passengers in the buses travelling between Sandwich and Ramsgate could be seen staring continuously at this remarkable addition to the landscape.

5

Trials

For eighteen months I had set myself hundreds of sailing puzzles: 'If the wind is out of the south-west at fifteen knots and the tide is ebbing, how will I pick up such-an-such a mooring? What preparations do I have to make to secure the boat singlehanded and what must I do if I miss the buoy on the first approach?' While travelling on trains, working on the boat or lying in bed I would put myself into every conceivable situation to see how quickly I could argue my way out of it. If the answer was not at my finger tips I would break out into a cold sweat while *Sir Thomas Lipton* ran on to the rocks and I struggled feverishly with my slothful brain. I was very much aware that my play-acting had yet to be put into practice, and whenever the word *trials* was mentioned, it was I who was intended for the rack, not my boat.

On Sunday, April 28th, Peter Bliss towed us down the Stour for our first sail. We had created a being which had his own personality, and as he made his first steps away from the dock a wave of elation swept over me and carried away the fears of sailing *Lipton* alone. The first few yards of movement in a boat after a long time away from the water are always memorable, and on this occasion they were made more so by the farewells from a group of people gathered on the quay.

At the entrance to Pegwell Bay we hoisted the boomed foresail and mizzen. The engine of the tug was so insulted by this manoeuvre that it promptly had a seizure, leaving us to pilot past the point under sail. We glided across the bay at four and a half knots while I hoisted the mainsail and jib. My first thought was, 'How slowly the boat is sailing.' When I looked at the log I was amazed to see it pointing to eight and a half knots, and it took me some time to get accustomed to not hearing the distant bow wave which is such a convenient aural log on a smaller boat. He seemed easy to handle and a delight to steer, and my hopes for the race soared. Derek Champ, his twelve-year-old-son, Robert, Brian Boots the bo'sun and John Perkins, a photographer from the *Weekend Telegraph*, were crew on this passage around to Cowes.

We spent the first day sailing round in circles off Ramsgate for the benefit of Anthony Howarth—another photographer from the *Telegraph*—and late in the afternoon set a course for the South Foreland. Dusk found us sailing peacefully past Dover harbour in those conditions which I came to love during the race: an over-cast sky, a swell rolling in from the south-west, a light wind and *Lipton* scything through the water at five knots with all his sails drawing. During the night the wind blew up to twenty-five knots and I was delighted to see that the decks stayed remarkably dry in the short sea. Some boats seem to sink into the water when they heel, but *Lipton* rolls out and pushes his weather side up at such an angle that a further eighteen inches of freeboard would not have improved the boat's dryness. Sailing past the Owers Light Vessel *Lipton* held a steady course for over an hour with the helm lashed, and on the way up the Solent Colonel Hasler's self-steering took over and proved to be a more competent helmsman than anyone on board. No one has yet steered *Sir Thomas Lipton* as well as the 'COLONEL'.

We were in good spirits as we sailed south towards the Shrape, half a mile east of Cowes harbour. I asked Robert how far we dared go on this tack, but my voice was drowned by the roar of a hovercraft flying west behind the boat. We sailed another hundred yards, tacked and started to sail parallel to, but fifty yards to the north of the red buoys marking the hovercraft lane. By this time the hovercraft had completed a semicircle and was flying back towards us from over the port bow. If the hovercraft continued its swinging turn we would be in the line of fire, but we all expected it to fly off at a tangent and keep inside the buoyed channel. By this time the hovercraft was the centre of attraction for the entire crew and we watched, hypnotised, as this flying dustbin lid came closer and closer.

I thought that the hovercraft's speed was about thirty miles per hour and *Lipton* was travelling at four knots which was too slow for evasive action. When I saw the expression on the pilot's face I was sure that a collision was inevitable and moved back from the port side of the deck. There was an almighty crash as the hovercraft hit us abeam of the mast and a shower of fibreglass fragments landed at our feet. Two port shrouds were carried away leaving the top half of the mast unsupported on the weather side and I fully expected the spar to crash down on the deck. We rushed forward to pull down the mainsail and jib while the hovercraft hissed in fury and deflated itself forty yards off our port quarter. It looked as if it was going to sink and I started to wonder how we could manoeuvre *Lipton* to pick up the survivors. Derek and Brian got the anchor ready, but we didn't need it because a launch that was ferrying workmen to a near-by boat came over to tow us into Cowes. The hovercraft recovered enough breath to blow itself up again and puffed its way into the harbour.

The next half hour was as extraordinary as the collision itself. When we reached the fore and aft moorings in Cowes harbour we were met by the Harbourmaster, Ben and John from Spencers and the foreman from Groves and Gutteridge's yard. The Harbourmaster heard about the collision over the radio and had gathered our repair team in less than fifteen minutes. Representatives from the hovercraft company came over to apologise for the accident and generously offered to pay for the damage. In no time at all Ben and John measured up the rigging screws, gave orders for the repair of the stanchions, checked the mast and the electric wiring. Everyone was full of sympathy, and without their energy in getting *Sir Thomas* on his feet again I could have been delayed for weeks instead of only four days.

Robert and I took stock of the situation over dinner and we decided that the outlook was far from bleak. The boat had exceeded all our expectations and promised to perform magnificently under the iron hand of the Colonel. The collision was further proof of the strength of the hull, for although two eight-ton cables were snapped off like match-sticks the hull had withstood the impact without a trace of damage. The accident gave me a much needed rest and I enjoyed four days of watching other people work instead of having to puzzle my own head.

The following Sunday we enjoyed the outstanding sail of the summer. The wind was south-westerly at twenty knots when we reached down to the Forts. Coming back up the Solent with *Lipton* held hard on the wind by the self-steering the log registered nine and a quarter knots for over half an hour. The wind was continually varying in direction as it puffed down from the island, but the self-steering followed the wind shifts so faithfully that it looked as if the wind direction indicator had stuck. This was the fastest that the boat had ever sailed on a course forty-five degrees off the wind.

Ever since the beginning of the project I had felt guilty about saying that I wanted to enter the singlehanded Transatlantic Race because I had never sailed a boat alone. I knew that as soon as *Lipton* was ready I would want to be off by myself, and when I went sailing with a crew I felt that I was cheating and would pretend that they were not there. During Sunday's sail I decided to set off the following Tuesday on my five hundred miles quali-fying passage. I had no qualms about the boat's ability, but I was plagued with worries about myself.

Lipton is a big boat to handle alone in crowded waters, and until I reached Newport I was in constant fear of colliding with another boat or losing control of the vessel. At that time it was the largest boat that had ever been sailed offshore by one man. But my worst fear was that tiredness, seasickness and lethargy would stop me driving the boat as hard and fast as his beautiful lines deserved. It would have been a crime to waste his theoretical speed by bungling on my part. For all of Monday I thought of nothing but the morrow's departure. When Brian Boots and I went ashore for a meal on Monday evening I looked around the restaurant with the eyes of a condemned man. How I envied the people at the bar. They could come back to this very place tomorrow evening. They would be drinking beer and swapping jokes while I was out there going through God knows what.

We retraced our steps to the dinghy and Brian had to keep waiting for me as I made the most of my last stroll on dry land. I cursed myself for ever having such romantic thoughts. I am a romantic not a sailor, and in taking my dreams to sea there had to come a time of reckoning. This was it and I was very frightened indeed. Why couldn't I have gone to some simple job tomorrow —oh dear—I would have put up with all sorts of drudgery to escape this creeping cancer that ate me out with apprehension. The realist side of my mind reminded the romantic department that I was in this blue funk precisely because I once imagined it would be good for me to be in this blue funk. So I had better get on with it.

I wanted every little mundane thing to take as long as possible. I rowed out to the *Lipton* at a pace that most people would call stationary and then made a great show of cleaning the galley.

Brian was soundly asleep before I finally produced the Horlicks. Within minutes he was snoring with a shrill trumpet-like bellow which continued to remind me for some hours of my plight. The considerable volume of Brian's nightly message was the last thing likely to keep me awake. The thoughts running through my head drowned Brian's exhortations with a thundering which would have awakened all of Cowes had I been able to give them voice. I did not sleep.

In the best R.A.F. tradition I had two eggs for breakfast while Brian gathered up his things and made arrangements to meet me in Falmouth at the weekend. Somehow, I could not bring myself to speak with any conviction when asked when and where I would like him to meet me. Meekly, I said that I had better telephone him, and I mused about my state of mind when I next saw Brian. I thought that I would be so relieved at completing the five hundred miles that anything less than a bear-hug at seeing him again would fail to match the occasion. Fortunately for all concerned I had quite forgotten my present state of mind by the end of the passage!

Tuesday morning was a total farce. We planned to set all *Lipton*'s sails, sweep in close to Cowes, let the sheets fly and gill along while we transferred Brian to the dinghy. While we were hoisting the sails the wash from a passing ferry boat doubling the height of *Lipton*'s wake managed to swamp the dinghy. For three hours we fought to keep the dinghy afloat and the full account of the gibes, oars lost and recovered, near drownings, amazed stares from passing boats, and Brian's heartfelt curses is a tale too sorry to be retold. Suffice to say that I was exhausted by the time the dinghy was buoyant again and very keen to get Brian off the boat so that I could get on with this accursed job that had to be done. I shouted to Brian to get into the dinghy and start rowing. I admit that I had not looked to see how far we were from the shore, and I could see in Brian's face all the desperation of a man being cast adrift in mid-Atlantic, for he is not the best oarsman in the world and we were a mile from Cowes with a full flood tide running to the east. He pleaded convincingly, and I steered *Lipton* towards the shore, half fearing that the dinghy would fill again. Luckily it didn't and Brian, soaked to the skin, looked very unhappy as he rowed away.

I ran off past Osborne Bay with the tide under me, and after setting the sails and adjusting the self-steering sat down in the cockpit to recover from the morning's excitements. *Lipton* seemed quite happy looking after himself and I had to admit that I was feeling less worried now that we were under way. I had expected to spend days, even weeks flitting about the boat in a nervous titter, but the morning's exercise had made me too tired for all that and immediately I settled into the same rhythm that I held all the way across the Atlantic. I had never dreamt that I would be preparing lunch in waters as restricted as the Solent, yet before passing the Horse Sand Fort, soup and rice pudding had been prepared and devoured. Half-way to the Nab Tower I was sandwiched between one of Thorensen's ferries half a cable to port and the *United States* a cable to starboard. If this had occurred in a pre-trials puzzle I would have been in a mental dither of action, adjusting this and checking that. Instead, I monitored my course on the cabin compass and kept an eye on proceedings by peeping through my perspex observation dome.

A Naval helicopter flew by and, surprised at seeing a ghost ship, came back to hover feet from the top of my mast. I played hookey by peeping out of my dome, and was amused to see the puzzled look on the pilot's face. Late in the afternoon the wind strengthened and I changed down to the number two jib without any difficulty.

Encouraged, I took a fifteen-minute nap before setting a southerly course. *Lipton* spun along at over eight knots for most of the evening and when I picked up the Barfleur light I tacked to the west. I didn't sleep during the night because there was too much shipping about, so I sat just inside the cockpit hatch or at my chart table and popped up every ten minutes to see what was going on.

The wind died away during the morning and I set the number one jib. For four hours we slopped about in a heavy swell with practically no wind. I made a note about changing the arrangement for the foreguys of the booms, took my first sunsight and some radio fixes. This confirmed my dead reckoning position twenty miles due south of Start Point. The wind filled in from the west during the afternoon and I set a course for a point about one hundred miles west of Ushant. If I sailed to this position and then back to Falmouth my log should read five hundred and ten miles.

Thursday brought welcome sunshine after Wednesday's drizzle and I reached my turning point at 15.36 and shaped a course for home. Only an hour before turning around I was still anxious about completing the passage safely, but as soon as I turned north towards Falmouth I felt that the voyage was as good as over. I have always noticed that I am more on edge before reaching the point of no return, and once the vessel is headed for home I start to drive the boat harder and with less concern. I had had three short naps since Monday night, and I knew that I could not sleep before reaching Falmouth since to oversleep would mean running blindly on to the coast.

After midnight the wind got up to over twenty-eight knots; but as it was abeam I did not change down. I blessed *Lipton*'s stiffness as he stood up to 1,170 square feet of canvas and screamed along at over ten knots. The self-steering worked magnificently and held the boat on a steady course despite the high seas rising under his counter. The noise was terrific, and I played the radio as loudly as I could to drown the tremendous thumps and bangs on deck. Every forty minutes or so I took a turn on deck to see that nothing was amiss and watched for shipping through the perspex dome. Just after four I saw the reflection of the Lizard Light on the underside of some low-lying cloud although I was still over forty miles from the lighthouse. I checked this bearing with my dead reckoning and changed course ten degrees to starboard. It seemed an age before the Lizard and Blackdown Head loomed out of the mist. By this time the wind had veered to the north of west and I hardened sail to hold my course into Falmouth. Just before nine o'clock I was half a mile off Pendennis Point but I had another eight miles to do before completing five hundred, so I tacked and headed back along my course.

It was still blowing hard so I decided to take down the number two jib and get the boat ready for picking up my mooring in the harbour. I moved forward on to the foredeck and let off the jib halliard. It ran off the winch for about eight feet and then went slack. Without looking up I heaved on the halliard and let it go again. It was still slack and I caught my breath as I realised what had happened. To reduce the load on the halliard winch we had arranged a two-part halliard with a block at the head of the jib. The halliard had jumped off the sheave of the block and jammed between sheave and cheek. No amount of pulling and tugging would lower the sail, and the only remedy was to climb the mast, swing out on to the stay and cut the halliard below the block.

I went aft and slumped into the cockpit to decide the best course of action. Everything had gone so well during the passage that it seemed almost inevitable that something should spoil it. I ate a handful of glucose tablets and decided that it would be safest to head the boat out to sea while I climbed the mast. The wire-cutters weighed sixteen pounds and were over four feet long so I strapped these to my back. Now that the halliard was slack, hard lines ran backwards from the luff of the sail and I was afraid it would tear. The anemometer read thirty knots as I hurried forward to get up the mast before the boat reached the rougher water beyond the shelter of the Lizard.

Although I had slowed the boat, the violent pitching threatened to throw me off the mast before I reached the spreaders. I trembled at the thought of what it would be like at the masthead when I would be travelling through an extra twenty-eight feet of arc every time the vessel dipped into a trough between the waves. Suddenly, I was aware of a roaring behind me and I clipped my harness to a shroud tang before twisting round to see a naval helicopter hovering behind my head. The roaring of the wind and crashing of the sea had drowned the noise of the helicopter until it was quite close. I gathered my breath for a few minutes, unclipped my harness and started climbing the mast steps above the spreaders. By this time I was beyond the shelter of the land and the sea became much rougher, and I saw that I had set the self-steering too close to the wind in trying to slow the boat and I was in danger of being put about. A large wave stopped *Lipton* in the eye of the wind and the jib started to flag mercilessly. Now it was a race to cut down the sail before it blew itself out and I scrambled up to the jumpers and hooked myself on again. The boat seemed to be pitching worse than ever, and as I surveyed the yawning gap between the head of the sail and the mast I realised that it would be folly to try to swing across it by holding on with the one hand and manipulating my giant wire cutters with the other. Already my forearms were crying with pain as I locked my arms around the spar and braced myself against the whip of the mast.

By this time the helicopter was hovering at my height fifty yards downwind of me. The pilot and crew members signalled simultaneously for me to get back on deck and I returned their good advice with a frozen stare of despair. Immediately I had decided to climb down from my perch there was a crack like the report of a rifle. The wind had blown out the clew of the sail. It took more than ten minutes for me to get back to the deck and once again I slumped into the cockpit to decide what to do.

Now the position was much more serious because I had no control over the jib which was acting like a massive air brake. It would be impossible for me to get on to my moorings in this pickle and the best I could hope for was to sail into the Carrick Roads, drop anchor on the North Bank in the lee of the high land behind Mylor and cut the sail down at my leisure. When I tried to tack I found that the flogging jib would not let *Lipton* sail close to the wind so I dared not let the boat fall off to the east of Falmouth, for if I did I would never get back. I had no choice but to stay at the tiller and guide the boat between Pendennis and St. Anthony and manoeuvre on to the North Bank without once sailing into the wind.

Normally I would have spent some time preparing and checking my ground gear, warps and tackle in readiness for anchoring but I did not dare to leave the tiller and I had to trust that all this was in order. It took over an hour to get the boat headed in the right direction, and I steered for the Pendennis side of the entrance knowing that I could always fall off to the east. The flapping of the sail was deafening, but even without this jib *Lipton* was close reaching at over seven knots. We swept between the headlands and I started the sheets and aimed for a point high on the Bank. Just when I judged the boat to be as high into the wind as she would sail I threw the sheets off the winches and dashed below.

If I failed to drop my fifty pound anchor within the minute *Lipton* would fall back to the deep main channel and would be pushed over to St. Just without a hope of sailing clear of the lee shore. The North Bank takes up most of the river, and if I was forced to anchor on the St. Just side of the channel I would be leaving no room for the boat to swing and I might be on to the rocks before the strain on the warp stopped the boat. The fore-hatches were open and in my panic I swung the fifty-pound anchor on to deck as easily as if it weighed a few ounces. I jumped up behind it, threaded the anchor through the pulpit and cast it clear of the bows. Already *Lipton* was paying off and falling back at a smart speed as I grabbed the warp and took two turns around the windlass. On the second turn I caught my thumb and fore-finger between the drum of the windlass and the warp, I knew the strain on the warp would crush my fingers and looked into the hatch to see if there was enough warp left for me to cast off these turns and take another. There was no warp to be seen and I found that I was holding the bitter end in my hand. I clearly remember asking myself which was the more important—thumb or boat. Shame made me cling like fury to the turns and I bit my lower lip so hard that it bled while the shock of the anchor biting home crushed my thumb. When the boat settled I heaved on the warp with my left hand and dragged my crushed fingers from the barrel. They had gone blue and white and were moulded into a shape that I did not remember seeing before.

The anchor held and I rushed aft to lower foresail, main and mizzen. Fearing that the kedge might give way I got the bower ready to throw over and then, with my right hand half useless, tied the wire-cutters to my back and reclimbed the mainmast. It was easy to get to the top when the boat was lying still, and in no time the accursed number two jib was sliding penitently down the stay. It was all over. I had done my five hundred miles.

Paul Williams's house looks out over the Carrick Roads. Pam had called him when she saw a ketch come into the harbour, but they both agreed that it could not be *Lipton* because he wasn't expected until Sunday. Paul looked through his binoculars, recognised the boat and dashed down to his dinghy. Now a dinghy came bouncing towards me and I recognised Paul crouching over the out-board. I have never been more pleased to see anyone. A few minutes later Frank Vinnicombe came chugging along in *Boy Willie* and I hailed him for a tow. I went below to attend to my fingers. Thankfully they were not broken. Frank towed us into Falmouth where the Harbourmaster helped us on to our moorings and in no time at all George Corke, Arfie Trenear and Bill Jennings appeared and we all settled down to a celebration whisky. I could not have been happier.

Here I was just two miles from my secret quay, sipping whisky with my sailing fathers on the new addition to the family, of which they obviously approved. The five hundred miles had taken two days twenty hours and this was the fastest qualifying time for the race. I had done the thing which had troubled my mind for so long and I would have been quite content not to sail again until June 1st.

6

Computer

In the same way that earnest young mountaineers have shocked the purists by using a battery of mechanical aids, and power-assisted gliders are annoying the old guard of the sailplane elite, so my computer invaded the sanctity of the yachting world. But how did a computer become involved? In ocean races with the R.O.R.C. it is common for a navigator to plot his own weather map to help him decide what course to steer. The steps in this operation are:

1. The Meteorological Office prepares its forecast in the form of a map.
2. This is encoded and transmitted at regular intervals as the shipping forecast.
3. The navigator interprets the shipping forecast and redraws the Meteorological Office's map, which is less accurate and less detailed than the original.
4. The navigator tries to predict the best course through the forecast pattern of weather.

It would be impossible to follow the same procedure for the Transatlantic Race because the forecast map is neither prepared in sufficient detail nor is it broadcast. Shipping forecasts which were arranged for the competitors were not sufficiently detailed for tactical navigation. Only a facsimile receiver would give me an accurate weather picture on board *Lipton*, but this would have been too expensive in terms of both electric current and cash.

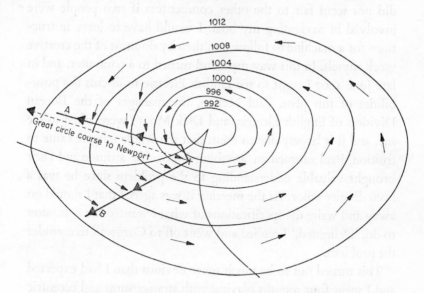

3. *Barometric Pressure Map I.* The tactical navigator dreams of exploiting situations like this. If he tacks north his boat will soon reach north-westerly winds and be able to lay a direct course for Newport. If he tacks south he will have to sail away from the shortest course to Newport for many hours before he can turn west.

The weather forecasts for the mid-Atlantic were not sufficiently detailed to give me this bird's eye view of the weather. The computer analysed the weather maps in London and chose the fastest route for me. The computer's answer was radioed to *Lipton* every morning.

On the other hand if my position was known in London it could be plotted on the original forecast map and the tactical navigation could be done more accurately. The answers could be radioed to me on board *Lipton*. But this raised the problem of how step four could be achieved. My first thought was to have another navigator who was well versed in the problems of tactical navigation do the work for me. I mused over this for some weeks and, quite apart from finding someone whose judgment I trusted, it did not seem fair to the other competitors if two people were involved in navigating my boat. I would have to leave instructions for a machine to follow and thereby do most of the creative work myself. In this way my mind turned to a computer, and in late June 1967 I went to see English Electric to discuss the possibilities of this plan. Paul McKee, the manager of the Bureau Division of English Electric, and Dick Moore were asked to see me, and it is largely due to them that the whole scheme came to fruition. Paul adopted an 'anything-is-possible' attitude and Dick brought valuable understanding to the problem since he was a keen dinghy sailor. At the meeting it was agreed that I should go away and write the specifications of what I wanted the computer to do. 'Delighted,' I replied and went off to Cornwall to consider the problem.

This turned out to be much more devious than I had expected and I spent four months playing with strange sums and eccentric figures before coming up with a tolerably satisfactory result. The difficulty was that the tactical navigator is totally intuitive in deciding what course to take, whereas I had to express the problem in a mathematical form. Later Ian Slater of English Electric and I went to confer with Meteorological Office representatives and we finally agreed on this plan:

(a) The K.D.F.9 computer at Bracknell would make up a forty-eight hour forecast map at about 5.30 a.m. each day. This was taken to the English Electric computer in Queensway and fed into another K.D.F.9 computer. I radioed my position to David Thorpe of the *Daily Telegraph* at 08.00 G.M.T. and he relayed this to English Electric. From my course and speed my position was advanced to 11.00 G.M.T. and this was fed into the computer to be crossed with the forecast map.

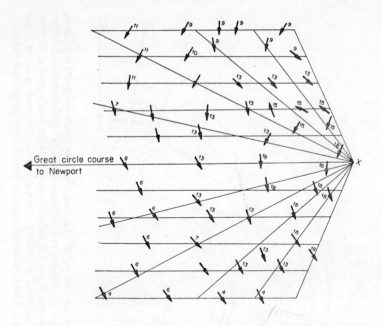

Great circle course
to Newport

X

4. The fan of courses with the values of wind speed and direction super-imposed on it. The computer can work out the angle between the direction of the wind and every one of these courses. At every point where a wind direction arrow crosses a course, the computer can work out the boat's speed at that point. It does this by applying the values of wind speed and 'angle of the true wind off the bow 'to the graphs shown in figure No. 5.

(b) The forecast map can be thought of as a grid with values of wind speed and direction scattered across it. Then all the possible routes that *Lipton* could take were cast on to the grid in the shape of a fan. The computer stored data of the boat's performance in the form of a number of polar curves. At every intersection of a possible course and a value of wind speed and direction, the computer worked out the boat's speed.

(c) This converted the fan of courses into a series of boat speeds which could easily be converted to give the total time required

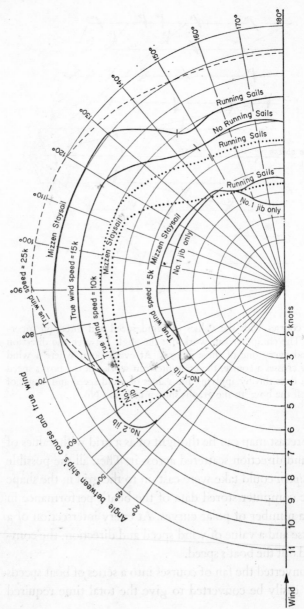

5. This set of graphs shows the speed of *Sir Thomas Lipton* on different points of sailing when the true wind speed is 5 knots, 10 knots, 15 knots and 25 knots. Note how powerful the boat is when going to windward at 50°–55° off the true wind. When the wind blows at 25 knots *Lipton* can reach at 11 knots. The mizzen staysail significantly improves the boat's speed at between 80° and 130° off the wind and the running sails can be set if the wind is within 30° of a dead run. The weakest sector of the boat's performance is between 140° and 160° off the true wind. This is where a spinnaker would be of the greatest value.

to sail along each course. Then the direction of the three shortest courses were radioed to me at 11.00 hours.

Geographical limits were imposed on the fan of courses by land and the Gulf Stream where it is strongest south of the American shore.

This system had the advantage of being the most accurate that was available; it meant that I did all my homework before the voyage and received the information in a convenient form with no more work to do other than make the final choice. To find out the value of this advice was the point of the experiment. I did not think that major deviations from the Great Circle Route could ever be fast enough to make up for the extra distance sailed so I intended to sail a Great Circle course with daily amendments made in the light of the computer advice. If the long-range weather forecast indicated a track other than the Great Circle course then I would bear this in mind when making my final daily choice of courses on *Lipton*.

Although computer course planning might give me a tactical advantage on only one or two days, this could win the race. But the problems of making all the arrangements for the exercise were trying to a degree. To feed the computer with the necessary data about the sailing performance of *Lipton* meant that my boat had to be fitted with the full range of Brookes and Gatehouse's instruments, and to transmit my position I had to install a powerful radio transmitter, electric wiring, aerials, batteries and a generating engine. When the difficulties surrounding the computer experiment began to mount in the last few weeks before the race I had a strong inclination to abandon the whole scheme and 'sail by the seat of my pants'. Then immediately, I would wonder if I was discarding a race-winning trump and English Electric's enthusiasm would win the day.

Difficulties with the installation of the radio transmitter dragged

6. 'Sir Thomas Lipton crossing the Atlantic', as seen by the French magazine Zero Un Informatit
The French were amused by the computer, the Americans were interested but the Briti
thought it wasn't quite cricket.

on and on and meant that I had to leave for Plymouth at the tenth hour, but a gale blew up from the south-east making it the eleventh hour on Monday, May 27th. The weather decided to be perverse and the southerly Force 4 which was forecast failed to show up and we spent twenty-one hours waiting for the wind to raise enough energy to send us to Plymouth. Mashford's sent a launch to Rame Head and we slipped at seven o'clock on Tuesday morning. The race committee allowed me to go to Mashford's boatyard because I was worried about a leak through the fairing between the hull and keel. Sid Mashford came aboard immediately, scrutineered the boat and went across to Plymouth on the ferry to report that my boat was fit and well. The fairing was not cracked but I was given a twelve-hour penalty for late arrival!

Tuesday and Wednesday were spent antifouling the bottom, and late on Wednesday we moved out to the buoys to make way for another competitor on the slip. That evening I went across to Millbay Docks to have a secret look at the other boats. There were crowds of people wandering around the dock which for one week every four years is turned into a haven for the practical dreamers. This year it was easy to see that some had dreamed too much and risked ending the race in prayer, while others had not dreamed enough and they would end up down the lists.

Drawings of the serious contenders in the race appear in the pages that follow. *Golden Cockerel* had capsized the year before and I thought that the memory of this could stop Bill Howell getting the most out of her during the race.

Cheers had just completed a 4,000-mile west to east crossing of the Atlantic in twenty-nine days and she looked a beautifully designed and carefully built craft. Even so, I did not give her much of a chance in a long beat to windward, and since the problems of singlehanded sailing in multihulls were less well known than in keel yachts I did not expect any of them to be first in Newport.

Of all the skippers in the race, I thought that Les Williams would be the hardest man to beat. He is a big, quiet chap who had been thinking about the race for some years. Although he was criticised for sailing a comparatively heavy boat with the largest working sails of any vessel in the race, I thought he was well able to cope. He only had two sails to worry about and this could have meant less work for him than would be necessary on *Raph* or *Sir Thomas Lipton*.

Voortrekker, the other boat from Van de Stadt's board, was too short on the waterline to win and was so light that I thought her fast motion in a seaway would make her a difficult boat to sail.

If I had been confronted by a facsimile of *Lipton* I would have been very worried indeed and the boat I feared most of all was *Raph* because she was most like my own. There were a number of points in *Raph's* design which gave me hope. In the first place she had not been designed specifically for the race and I believed that anything less than this was courting failure. Her gear was arranged for offshore racing in the traditional manner, with very little thought given to the demands of this race. *Raph* looked a difficult boat to tack, her low-cut genoa would be more cumbersome to handle than one with a high clew; there were no running sails and, although she was heavier than *Lipton*, she had less sail area. She was trimmed down by the stern and Alain was full of worry about his rudder. In fact he beached *Raph* at Mashford's the next day and removed the rudder from the boat. If major operations were being carried out so late, I wondered how much minor surgery had been neglected. Despite these handicaps, *Raph* was the longest monohull that had been entered and if the record of the previous races was maintained, then she should win.

As the day of the start grew closer the same symptoms of fear that I had known at Cowes came back to rack me again. I dreaded the weeks of sleepless action that were to come and longed with all my heart to stop the clocks, to put off the awful hour and give myself time to rest and prepare my mind. For me it would be impossible to cross the Atlantic singlehanded without months of mental preparation, and although I had been thinking about a singlehanded passage for years, I still craved for a longer lull before the gun. It would have been easy if it were a cruise across the Western Ocean, but this race would stretch me continuously, never letting me relax, never letting me forget the hundreds of people who had put energy, money and trust in *Lipton*, never letting his bows look away from Newport, U.S.A. It would have been easy if I had been sailing with a crew; then I would not, by way of preparation, have to push aside those who were closest to me for what was to come.

During the last three days the mundane things of life assumed a new and joyful significance. Mealtimes were oases of pleasure to distract a taut mind from the impending trial. The sea mist, the skies and the woods behind the boatyard at Cremyll assumed a loveliness so overpowering that it was as if I had been almost blind to them before. Their colours were deeper and richer, their shapes more sensuous, their perspective more clearcut and I mourned my leaving them.

7

The Start

I will never forget June 1st, 1968. I woke up just after six o'clock
and went into the cockpit to look at the weather. It was one of
those dull days with a low overcast sky which promised drizzle
before the dew-covered decks had had time to dry. The wind was
nowhere and I mused about the possibilities of our start being
becalmed. The thought of fiddling with kedge anchors against the
tide didn't fill me with joy and I went below to listen to the
weather forecast. This hinted at westerlies within forty-eight
hours and I was grateful for that, but the chance of collision and
catastrophe in the Sound left me weak with apprehension. I made
some coffee and spread honey on bread, but the very sight of it
crystallised all the fears that were gripping me and I was sick
into a red plastic bucket. Not a good wholesome kind of sickness
with ships of meat floating in a brown gravy, but a mean, acid
sickness offering up a green liquid which scalded the throat and
the mouth and lent no sweating release from worry and discomfort.

At times of crisis my bowels can be relied upon to show their
sympathy with any other afflicted organ by throwing a fit of
diarrhoea. For an hour, diarrhoea and nausea played a ridiculous
symphony on *Sir Thomas Lipton's* one-man band and I made
weary circuits from sitting on the red bucket to jettisoning it into
the Tamar to looking into the red bucket and back to the Tamar
again until I felt as if I had run ten miles.

9. At that time it was the largest boat that had ever been sailed offshore by one man.

10A. *Lipton* going to windward at 9 knots with remarkably low bow and quarter waves.

10B. (*left*) The self-steering gear was designed by Colonel H. G. Hasler. It keeps the boat sailing at a constant angle relative to the direction of the wind. When the boat wanders off course this angle changes and the wind vane lines itself up with the new wind direction. This movement of the wind vane turns the fore-and-aft line of the servo blade which is hanging in the water. As soon as the width of this blade turns at an angle to the water rushing past the boat it tries to swing to port or starboard. The blade is allowed to swing to either side because it is mounted on a swivel at deck level. On top of the blade is a quadrant (see photo) which must turn in the opposite direction to the swing of the blade. Nylon lines are attached to the quadrant and run through blocks to the tiller. So when the blade swings, it turns the quadrant which pulls on the tiller and brings the boat back to its original heading relative to the wind.

10C. Some boats seem to sink into the water when they heel, but *Lipton* rolls out and pushes his weather side up at such an angle that a further eighteen inches of freeboard would not have improved the boat's dryness.

Paul and Bill were moored along-side and they came on board to help with last-minute jobs. They were quieter than usual and we were all glad to be diverted by the antics of Bill Howell. He was towed out of Mashfords by the yard launch and swept by, sporting a multicoloured umbrella and quaffing cans of beer. He was in the best of spirits and cracked jokes with everyone he saw. Bill and Paul exchanged glances, and I imagined they were thinking that they had a very sick child on their hands.

Paul and I discussed tactics for the start. Although the weather called for the 1,020 square foot ghoster this was set on the outermost forestay and I would have to do a Chinese gibe if I wanted to tack. Such a manoeuvre was not recommended for Plymouth Sound. We settled for the number one jib. Robin Curnow came on board and Bill went back on *Tilly Witch*. We set the jib in stops, got our warps ready and unfurled the boomed sails while we waited for Sid Mashford to come back with the launch. I had a last look at the chart, noted bearings and tides, went back on deck and sat glumly on the perspex dome. At a quarter to ten, Sid drew alongside and we made fast to his transom. There was a good deal of empathy between the Mashfords and *Lipton* because we shared Cornwall and a love for keel yachts as opposed to the three-legged monsters that had come to their yard from foreign parts. *Lipton* tows easily and we motored downstream past the Drake's Island and Millbay Docks. The wind was still on holiday. The forecast said it would fill in from the south, so I chose the eastern end of the starting line and dropped my kedge anchor. At the briefing there had been a lot of confused talk about anchoring in the starting area, and it was still not clear where we were permitted to anchor and for how long. In ordinary yacht races we would not be allowed to moor on the starting line after the ten-minute gun, but then, this was no ordinary yacht race.

Paul and Robin hoisted the boomed sails and *Lipton* rode to the tide with the canvas flapping listlessly. There was an armada of spectator boats and the Navy seemed to be doing a good job of controlling them. Two Marines roared up in a high speed motor-boat to deliver telegrams and a weather map. I think that Paul and Robin must have been feeling like unwelcome guests who had turned up at the wrong party and they were both looking around for someone to ferry them ashore. Luckily, Johnny Coote saw their plight and piloted a 10-ton auxiliary yacht alongside to let Robin swing on to its deck. I turned to Paul and complained of nerves. He gripped my hand, looked straight down at me and said that anyone would be nervous before 'this lot'. Then he was gone.

Alone at last. I slipped my buoyed anchor before the ten-minute gun and spent fifteen minutes wearing the boat around to the west. It took an age to drift to the end of the breakwater and *Lipton* barely had steerage way. At one moment I was on a collision course with *Silvia II* and was unable to tack away from her because *Coila* was at my other side. As we handed each other off, Foezon muttered something in French and I was glad that I could not understand him.

Near the breakwater, *Lipton* started to drift slowly towards an anchored dinghy. There was nothing I could do to avoid him and I prayed hard that he would be able to get his anchor up in time. When I was ninety yards off he heard me shout and watched with growing anxiety as I got larger and his anchor seemed to get no lighter. At last, he had it on board and the current carried him along in front of me. Luckily the outboard started at the first pull and he slipped safely away from my shark-like bow. A friend hailed me derisively from another spectator boat. He had never heard me mention sailing when we were at Oxford together, and he was perplexed about the whole show. 'Why aren't you going faster?' he cried. I was in no mood for jest, could think of no suitable reply and returned his question with a sulky stare. I craved to be free of the Sound and to be away from the spectator boats which were churning up the water and upsetting the momentum of the yacht.

I was lying nineteenth as *Lipton* left Rame Head on the starboard hand, and I kept telling myself that a drifting match was no indication of the other vessels' speeds. Nevertheless, I was most surprised at the way the multihulls—particularly *Pen Duick IV* and *Cheers*—had coped with the light going, as I had expected them to be the inferior performers in these conditions. At three-thirty in the afternoon I was still only two and a half miles outside the breakwater with *Myth of Malham*, *Voortrekker*, *Ocean Highlander* and *Rob Roy* all less than four hundred yards away. We were all heading straight for the Lizard on a course that took us away from the shore. To the north I could see *Raph*, *Spirit of Cutty Sark*, *Cheers*, *Coila* and *Jester* with her lugsail, all going faster than our group. I had thought that with such an overcast sky and drizzle forecast for most of the day there would be little or no land breeze to warrant sailing along the coast.

Now the sun was trying to break through a thin cloud cover and I reckoned it would be worth while sailing off to the north-west. After forty minutes an area of catspaws showed up ahead and I altered course again to stay in this light breeze yet make a better heading for the Lizard. These were the sailing conditions that I love most of all. The wind was blowing from the south-west at five knots and the boat was sailing perfectly over a flat sea. The breeze was kicking up ripples no more than two inches high and it was the grandest sensation to feel *Lipton* scything through this grass at four knots with the self-steering gear cutting a perfect course and fifteen hundred square feet of sail doing exactly what it should do. About five miles to the north I could just see the day beacon at Fowey and five miles to the south *Pen Duick IV* was

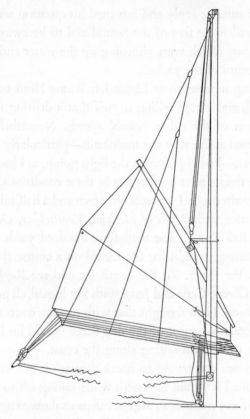

7. *Jester's* reefed lugsail

Although this design is based on principles well tried by the Chinese, it is a novelty in Western waters. The advantage of this arrangement for singlehanded sailing is that it is possible to reef right down in about a minute without going on deck. All the sheets and halliards can be handled from a single circular control hatch in *Jester's* deck. The mast is unstayed and the heaviest line used as a sheet or halliard is $\frac{3}{4}''$ in circumference and the sail cloth weighs 6 oz. per square yard. *Jester* has made five passages across the Atlantic as well as a return trip to the Azores and she has never experienced a gear failure of any consequence. Although the rig is not particularly close-winded, this is comparatively unimportant for ocean voyaging.

tacking, tacking and tacking again without making much progress.

Les Williams had got right away, but I soon overhauled *Coila* and was keeping pace with *Cheers* when I was startled by a shout from the port quarter. Alain Gliksman in *Raph* had crept silently up behind me after the last tack and was now sailing level with *Lipton* and barely fifty yards away. Although I had had very little contact with the competitors I did feel a strong link of camaraderie with them. I had seen more of Alain than any of the others and I was pleased to see him again. We shouted to one another and we were happy to enjoy some company before the solitude that was to come. If there are moments in sport when two people of different countries and personalities are united through a common goal in understanding and respect, then this was such a time. Alain was scampering about on deck adjusting his sails and tampering with his self-steering. He looked tanned, fit and happy, which was such a contrast to the worried man I had seen examining his rudder at Mashfords. *Raph* and *Lipton* sailed together for about an hour. *Lipton* was pointing slightly higher and going at the same speed. Soon we were out of earshot and I tacked to the west. I distinctiy remember sitting back in the cockpit and suddenly feeling swamped by a wave of euphoria. It felt as if the worried mask I had been wearing for the past nine months was swept away and I smiled despite myself. I am sure that colour came back into my face as I realized that all the hectic preparations were over and I had won the race to Plymouth. There would be no more telephone calls, no more bills, no more well-wishers and no more crises to prevent me taking part in the race. At teatime I was happier than I had ever been and this state of mind lasted for twenty-five days.

Length overall   67' (20·4 m.)   Length waterline   59·7'   (18·1 m.)
Beam   35' (10·7 m.)   Draft   3·9'   (1·19 m.)
Displacement   4·9 tons   Sail area   1284 sq. ft.   (119·8 sq. m.)
Owner: Eric Tabarly. *Designer*: J. Rouillard. *Builders*: Chantier et Ateliers de la Perrière,
Lorient.

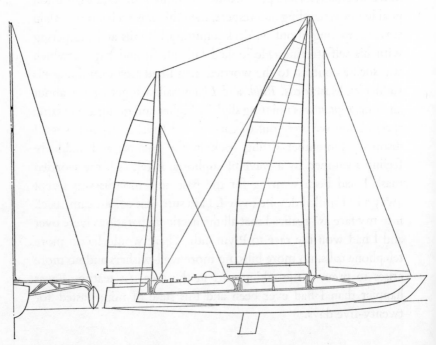

8B. *Pen Duick IV:* Sail plan

72

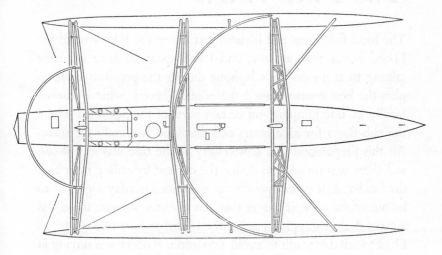

8B. *Pen Duick IV:* Arrangement

There are very few multihulls which 'look right' and the three most striking exceptions—*Pen Duick IV*, *Gancia Girl* and *Cheers*—were entered for the 1968 race. Of these, *Pen Duick IV* was the most revolutionary. This ocean racing boat incorporated features which had only previously been seen on inshore racing catamarans. These included a rotating mast of aerofoil section, fully battened sails, main and mizzen sheet tracks which described complete semi-circles, and centre boards with very limited lateral area. The outriggers were narrow in the bows and this may have been intended to stop the vessel 'tripping' at high speed. This two-berth boat was built of aluminium alloy and was neither painted not antifouled for the race. The sail plan shows no overlapping between the foresails and the mainsail which means there could be no slot effect. Despite her size she must have been one of the easiest boats to handle because she had a comparatively small sail area and a more or less horizontal working platform. After the race the aerofoil mast was discarded.

73

8

The First Week

The local fishermen and lifeboatmen know the tides around the Lizard better than anyone, and I had spent an hour or more talking to them on the telephone during the previous week to plan the best course around the point. There is what is known locally as 'tide jumping' off certain parts of the peninsula where the ebb flows for nine hours and the flood lasts only for three. All this preparation was unnecessary as the tide was in full ebb and there was no need to dodge the current by sailing in behind the headland. It was impossible to sleep on Saturday night, or to be out of the cockpit longer than ten minutes, because there was a great deal of shipping passing the Lizard and on two occasions I had to sail due south to avoid a collision. Robert was staying at the Housel Bay Hotel and I knew that Father and Dobs, my stepmother, planned to join him for a drink at about ten. Little did they know that I was passing less than a mile and a half away. I was tempted to call them on the radio telephone. During the night the wind went around to the north-west and blew more strongly.

Sunday, June 2nd

At first light *Myth of Malham* showed up a cable to leeward. It was quite cold and I sat huddled in the cockpit and watched her skipper, Noel Bevan, change down from number one to number two jib. His big genoa staysail kept pulling during the

11. THE COMPETITORS, 1968 SINGLEHANDED TRANSATLANTIC RACE

Top Row, left to right

Bill Howell (Australia) *Golden Cockerel*
Bruce Dalling (S. Africa) *Voortrekker*
Bernard Rodriquez (U.S.A.) *Amistad*
Tom Follett (U.S.A.) *Cheers*
Michael Richey (U.K.) *Jester*
Geoffrey Williams (U.K.) *Sir Thomas Lipton*
William Wallin (Sweden) *Wileca*
Edith Baumann (W. Germany) *Koala III*
Mike Pulsford (U.K.) *White Ghost*
I. L. R. Williams (U.K.) *Spirit of Cutty Sark*
Eric Willis (U.K.) *Coila*

E. Heinemann (W. Germany) *Aye-Aye*
Claus Hehner (W. Germany) *Mex*
Eric Tabarly (France) *Pen Duick IV*
L. Paillard (France) *La Delirante*
Commandant B. Waquet (France) *Tamoure*
Sandy Munro (U.K.) *Ocean Highlander*
André Foezon (France) *Sylvia II*

Middle Row, left to right

Joan de Kat (France) *Yaksha*
N. S. A. Burgess (U.K.) *Dogwatch*
Rev. S. W. Pakenham (U.K.) *Rob Roy*
Noel Bevan (U.K.) *Myth of Malham*

Capt. H. J. Minter-Kemp (U.K.) *Gancia Girl*
B. de Castelbajac (France) *Maxine*
Alex Carozzo (Italy) *San Giorgio*
Lt. B. Enbom (Sweden) *Fione*
Colin Forbes (U.K.) *Startled Faun*
R. G. M. Wingate (U.K.) *Zeevalk*
B. T. A. Cooke (U.K.) *Opus*
Alain Gliksman (France) *Raph*
M. Cuiklinski (France) *Ambrina*

In Front

J. Ives Terlain (France) *Maguelonne*
Ake Mattisson (Sweden) *Goodwin II*
Guy Piazzini (Switzerland) *Gunther III*

12. It took an age to drift to the end of the breakwater. *Lipton* barely had steerage way.

The start, with the fleet edging its way past Plymouth Breakwater. We were all worried about starting the race inside Plymouth Sound and we were lucky that the wind was so light.

No 32 *Aye-Aye*, sailed by Egon Heinemann.
No 37 *Sylvia 11*, André Foezon.
No 30 *Startled Faun*, Colin Forbes.
No 17 *Wileca*, William Wallin.
No 34 *Gunther 111*, Guy Piazzini.
No 38 *Mex*, Claus Hehner.
No 14 *Opus*, Brian Cooke.

14. *Jester* off Rame Head.

sail change and the boat seemed to lose very little speed when he was sailing bareheaded. I had changed down just before dawn and it seemed an age before I overhauled the *Myth*. She was sailing beautifully. *Lipton* passed close to the Wolf Rock Light-house and I shaped a course for the northern tip of Round Island. The tide was setting strongly to the east and with the wind blowing up to Force 6 from the north-north-west I had to keep a wary eye on the proceedings and make sure that I was not forced too close to the lee shore of Round Island. Although *Lipton* was sailing at seven and a half knots the tide took its toll and it was ten o'clock before we were clear of the Scillies. For most of Sunday I was watching for Bob Lewis's light aircraft. He had planned to bring Father out to look for me, but there was nothing in sight.

Most people imagine that singlehanded sailors catch their breath and expect the worst when they leave the shelter of the shore. Not true, the open sea means safety, not danger. Here there is much less risk of being run down by a freighter than in restricted channels and it is a great comfort to know that one can afford to run before a gale in any direction without being wrecked on the shore.

Once clear of the Scillies I set about calling David Thorpe of *The Daily Telegraph*. I let the transmitter warm up and started calling on the distress frequency 2182 k.c.s., 'This is yacht *Sir Thomas Lipton*, yacht *Sir Thomas Lipton*, yacht *Sir Thomas Lipton* calling Land's End radio, come in please.' I had only had a couple of hours to practise with the radio telephone before the race and there had not been time to issue a proper call sign, but remember-ing all the excitement that had surrounded *the* Sir Thomas Lipton's life and his challenges for the America's Cup, I was more than a little proud to be using his name as my call signal. 'Yacht *Sir Thomas Lipton* stand by on 1841 k.c.s. and call me on 2555 k.c.s.' I marvelled at the fact that this grey box and its attendant cat's cradle of wires, aerials and insulators actually worked, and I switched the transmitter and receiver to working frequencies. There must have been a lot of traffic because I had to wait five minutes before the radio station came back on the air to ask for the telephone number I wanted. I was two hours late calling David and he was obviously pleased to hear me. I was able to pass my messages as easily as in a normal telephone conversarion. When Round Island was dipping below the horizon I had my first sleep. Ninety minutes later I was woken by the off-course alarm and spent the rest of the day and night napping for a few minutes at a time between watching the boat's progress. I was feeling too sick to eat very much but managed a few raisins and some chocolate.

Monday, June 3rd

Monday broke with the news that Tabarly was returning to Plymouth for repairs to his mizzen mast. Ironically he had been sighted by Bob Lewis who had set out to look for me. At 0080 hours G.M.T. I called David again and gave him the necessary data for the computer to work out its courses:

50°05'N, 9°54'W. Course 230°. 6 knots. Wind—westerly at 9 knots. Barometer steady 30", 55°F, Sunny.

Three hours later I called the English Electric office in Queensway and spoke to Dick Moore who gave the following information:

Course 305°, change to 279° late tonight.

I expected to be given three courses but supposed that this answer had been given by the computer for the second and third choice.

It was always left to me to choose the exact course to follow in the light of conditions at the ship. The picture of long-range weather forecast analogues was very vivid in my mind, and these showed a close grouping of isobars along the loxodromic route and more widely spaced isobars and weaker winds on or north of the Great Circle route. I put more trust in the analogues than the Meteorological Office thought was wise.

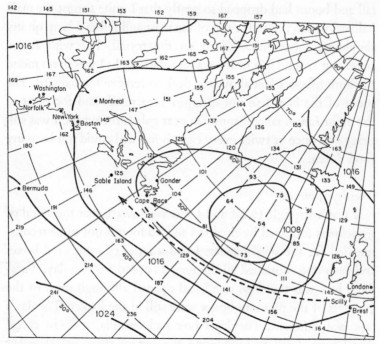

9. *Barometric Pressure Map II.* One of the analogue maps (1965) used to prepare the long range forecasts for the first half of June 1968. Winds promised to be lighter and freer on the northern course.

The boat's course over the first two or three days of the race is more important in shaping the overall pattern than daily courses two or three weeks later and I was keen to get north to avoid the strong winds forecast south of the Great Circle route.

The wind blew out of the north-north-west at twenty knots until midday when it fell off to less than ten. *Lipton* drove along at six knots despite a confused and lumpy sea.

All day the sky was overcast and I felt sick. By nightfall the wind rose to twenty-five knots and I went forward to drop the mainsail on deck. I was feeling so pleased with myself that the sail and boom had dropped so neatly that I quite forgot the main halliard which ran to the top of the mast and fell in a heap on my shoulders. I had intended to set the trysail, but with *Lipton* bouncing around in a heavy sea on a dark night I was in no mood to climb fifty-six feet above the deck to rereeve the halliard. The speed of the boat had not dropped very much and for most of the night *Lipton* sailed happily in near gale force winds. I was still being sick once or twice every eight hours and could not keep my food down.

Tuesday, June 4th

It was a struggle to eat and I was well aware that the spiral of seasickness followed by tiredness and no food is not to be recommended for the singlehander. I had a series of numbered boxes and each one contained all the food I needed for one day. Tuesday's box was the third one I had opened although most of the contents of the previous boxes were still in the locker. Tuesday's box was different. Tuesday's box had Familia, a Swiss cereal that I love. I fell to plundering the rest of the neatly labelled packages and within minutes my carefully planned diet was ravished of its strategic offerings of the magical Familia. The sickness abated.

By dawn the wind had dropped enough for the boat to miss its mainsail and I tried to get to the top of the mast. There was still a heavy sea tossing *Lipton* about and it took ten minutes to get as high as the spreaders. The rolling of the boat made climbing the mast difficult, and every time the vessel pitched I would be thrown forward and whipped around the ratlines. The higher I climbed the worse the motion became and I dared not go above the spreaders. I would have to wait until the seas calmed down and try again. In the meantime I put in my morning call to David Thorpe. I remembered that when I was tying down my halliards at Mashfords I was interrupted by a well-wisher and when I came back to the job I went past the main halliard thinking it had been done. Under my breath I muttered rude things about the visitor and offered him the job of climbing the mast. He did not take it up. At half past ten I tried again and managed to reach the top and clip the safety harness to a tang while I rerove the halliard.

Tuesday was gloomy with windward work throughout the day. Late in the afternoon the boat unexpectedly came head to wind and tried to go off on the other tack. I scrambled back on to the counter to find that a screw in the self-steering mechanism was missing. Luckily it did not affect the working of the gear, but it would prevent me setting the attitude of the windvane to the wind direction by the remote guide lines that fed into the cockpit. This was a bore, but not critical. On the evening news I heard that Bruce Dalling had lost his boom and in my own mind I wrote him off from the race. How wrong I was!

I had no sleep all night because the off-course alarm kept ringing. The wind was varying its direction every twenty minutes or so, and I was continually called on deck to change the boat's heading and reset the sails.

Wednesday, June 5th

Wednesday was another dull, overcast, gloomy day with moderate to fresh winds coming from the direction I was trying to go. I took comfort from my discomfort by reasoning that this was the weather the monohulls needed. This was the first day

RAPH

Length overall	57·4′ (17·5 m.)	Length waterline	42·5′ (13·0 m.)
Beam	13·4′ (4·1 m.)	Draft	8·2′ (2·5 m.)
Displacement	12·8 tons	Sail area	1042 sq. ft. (94·85 sq. m.)

Skipper: Alain Gliksman. *Designer*: André Mauric. *Builder*: A.C.N.A.M.

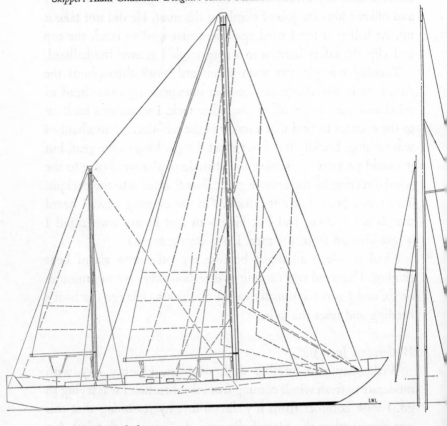

10A. *Raph*: Sail plan

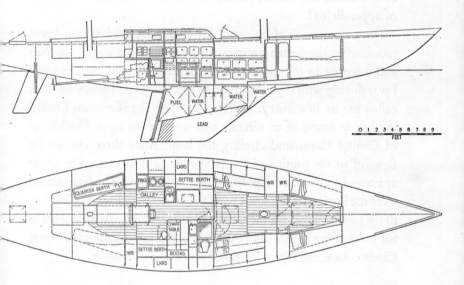

OB. *Raph*: Arrangement

Raph was built of aluminium some 50 miles south of Paris and trucked to the sea shortly before the race. It has been designed more for offshore racing than singlehanded sailing and the influence of the rating rule makes it a very different boat from *Sir Thomas Lipton*. The main points of difference are the pinched ends of the hull, less sail area although *Raph* weighs a $\frac{1}{2}$ ton more than *Lipton*, much higher freeboard, low cut head sails, six versus three winches in the cockpit and no arrangements for running downwind for the solo skipper. The designer has concentrated on keeping the weight in the boat as central and as low as possible.

that I had been able to eat breakfast, and I followed this with a morning's work checking right through the boat. I ran the charger for three hours, tried to stem the leaky forehatches, baled the bilge water into a bucket and tipped it into the self-draining cockpit. This method seemed quicker than using the bilge pumps. On deck the foresails needed repacking in their sausage skins and some nuts needed tightening on the self-steering. At lunchtime I was sick again and this time it was accompanied by sharp pains in the lower right hand side of my stomach. Immediately I feared the worst; perhaps the sickness was the forerunner of appendicitis!

For most of the afternoon I lay in the leeward saloon berth monitoring the boat's progress by watching the ship's compass and listening to the ticking of the electromagnetic log. As usual I was dozing with my oilskins on in case some emergency on deck called me up in a hurry. Halfway through the afternoon I heard the heavy drone of an aircraft and went up to see a Shackleton of Coastal Command circling the boat. After three circuits he flew off to the south and I watched to see if he started to circle again and show me the position of another boat. He disappeared over the horizon and I went back to my sickbed. I was feeling too ill for food and was glad when the boat sailed on without attention for most of the night. My heading was still just north of the Great Circle course and *Lipton* averaged seven knots all night.

Thursday, June 6th

Before the morning's transmission I sat for over an hour at the chart table wondering what news there would be and how I was doing compared with the other boats. The Shackleton would have reported the positions to the race committee, and I expected David to know the worst. His first news was that Tabarly had retired. I knew how much he wanted to win the race for the

15A. *Lipton* is a stiff vessel and this is a typical angle of heel when going to windward in a 15 knot wind.

15B. The computer team. (*left to right*): John Meaker, Jennifer Lawrence, Ian Slater, Dick Moore and the KDF9 in the background.

16A. *Cheers:* a beautifully built and inexpensive proa. For stability it relies on keeping the outrigger to leeward so that when it tacks, the masts and booms must revolve and the boat goes off in the other direction. The jib must be taken down and hoisted on the 'new bows' and a second rudder is dropped into the water to steer the boat. *Cheers* is so well balanced that she does not need a self-steering gear.

16B. The cabin of *Cheers*. The photographer is sitting on a bunk which completes the accommodation!

second time. I knew how empty and vague life would seem before he could set his sights on something else. I asked David to tell him 'Hard luck'. *Raph* was forty miles south of me with ten miles more westing and the other boats were spread out behind us. This was encouraging news because for the past three days with the wind mainly from the north-west to north-north-west it would have been much easier to free off and go faster by steering the more southerly course which *Raph* had followed. I had been hard on wind, and as I was only a few miles behind *Raph* it meant that my boat was every bit as fast, if not faster than Alain's.

During another day of beating to windward in continuous drizzle I began to feel better physically, but worse mentally. I had just heard that Bobby Kennedy was dead and this threw a pall of depression across the boat which lasted for some days. Late in the afternoon I chocked myself into the galley and tried to cheer myself up by preparing a huge tea of sardines on toast, raisins, rice and tea. I was halfway through this feast when there was a high-pitched scream that had me scuttling on to the deck fully expecting to see a liner bearing down on me with both propellers set in reverse. Instead, a twin-engine French aircraft was buzzing *Lipton* at mast-height. First of all he came in from astern on a run that was so low that I was involuntarily ducking as I crouched in the cockpit. Far from feeling pleased to see somebody else I was annoyed at being disturbed, and went below to get on with high tea. The aircraft continued to run low over the ship and I watched idly through my dome. I think I resented this intrusion into my little world because the crew of the plane would be back in France within a couple of hours. That evening they would be able to go to the cinema or meet their friends for a meal while I would still be cooped up in my low cabin. It was not that I didn't like it at sea; I did. But while I was in the race

I did not want to be reminded of shoreside pleasures and I hoped that the plane would soon fly away taking with it the image of normal life.

Friday, June 7th

By ten o'clock the wind had died away to ten knots and although stronger winds were forecast for later in the day I decided to set the seven hundred square feet jib. The number two is very easy to get down when the wind goes light and I had the number one drawing within half an hour of leaving the cockpit. This is a very long time compared with an efficient sail change on an ocean racer, but it was good by my standards.

Three hours later I noticed that the saloon berth where I was lying became more comfortable. This was because the boat started to heel more steeply and I was cradled more firmly in the L-shape of the Pirelli webbing. I knew that the speed picked up from six knots to over seven knots by counting the number of ticks per minute on the electromagnetic log. I reached up and pulled down the compass to see if we were still on course. Five degrees to starboard. 'Well, that's all right, just remember to enter that up when I write the log,' I said to myself. Ten minutes went by without incident. Then the banging started . . . .

The log has climbed to seven and a half knots, *Lipton* is showing off by dancing from one wave to the next only to be brought to his senses by an almighty crash. But he is slow to learn and does it again. And again. And again. Then the forehatches start to drip which means that water is sweeping across the foredeck. I suppose I had better have a look. I reach up and grab the hand-rail, throw my damp blue blanket on to the top berth and peep through the dome. The sky looks darker and the sea has got rougher. I look across to the instruments. Speed—O.K. Heading —O.K. I note change of course in log. Everything looks all right for the moment and I slip back to my bunk. Another half hour passes and then, in the space of five minutes, there is a series of four crashes that slows the boat by a knot. I get out of my bunk again and take a peep at the weather from the cockpit hatch. The sky looks black and ugly and water is bubbling along the lee rail. *Lipton* is heeling too much and not going so fast. I will have to change down. This is the worst sail change of all because I have to cope with the ship's largest working sail in the most exposed part of the boat when the vessel is heeling at his maximum. It is much easier to take in a smaller sail in a whole gale than it is to get in the number one jib when it is blowing at eighteen knots.

My waterproof jacket hangs just inside the hatch on the port side. As I put it on over my high P.V.C. trousers I start to work out the order of things on deck. No matter how tired I might have been five minutes ago in my bunk, the thought of working on the foredeck banishes all weariness and starts to pump the adrenalin around my system. If anything is likely to go wrong it is during a sail change and I have always disliked working in the wet on a quick moving foredeck. It is so much easier to work back by the mast or in the cockpit. I wrap a towel around my neck, but I don't pull the hood up because I like to be able to hear and sense what is going on just behind my head. The cockpit is cold and wet after the muggy cabin and I check that the sheets are ready to run out and that the tails are flaked down without any tangles.

Now it's time to move slowly and carefully along the weather guard rails to the foredeck. Whenever possible I like to work sitting down with my leg twisted around a winch and one arm crooked around a stay. I lace myself into position by a winch on the foredeck and sort out the fall of the halliard. It has been neatly coiled and lashed to the winch but it must be flaked down into a heap to be sure that it will run off without a hitch. When this is done I let off all the turns from the halliard winch except the last one which holds the sail. I lie back and check the sail aloft and see how the halliard is setting through its blocks. It seems to be pulling over one of the boom slides and I crawl back to the mast to clear it.

As soon as I get back to the mainmast the spray stops drenching me. I continue back to the counter. Reaching up, I grab the vane and line it up about thirteen degrees off the centre-line of the ship. This is enough to bring the boat up into the wind but not so much that he gets caught in irons. The jib starts to flap and I must rush forward to the halliard winch again before there is any chance of it being backed. One turn cast off the winch and the halliard starts to run. The sheet has not been released so the sail falls within reach of the foredeck. Now I must crawl up ahead of the forestay and pull the luff of the sail down the stay, but as I crawl over the sail which has already fallen to the deck, a stronger gust of wind catches the jib and rushes it back up the stay. I am whipped off my feet and feel myself rising in the belly of the sail. I grab desperately for the guard rail and fall back to the deck with a bump.

Little incidents like this frighten me more than anything and chastise me for leaving this sail set for so long. I manage to scrape forward of the forestay and pull the sail down as far as it will go. Then I tie down the head of the sail with a nylon strap and move back down the leeward side, pulling the sail inboard as I go. Back on the counter again the self-steering is reset and the boat is gathering way again by the time I am in the cockpit. The sheet is thrown off and let run for about twelve feet. Back to the foredeck again and the sheets are untied from the clew of the sail and made fast on the stanchions. The sausage skin is unlaced and I spend twenty minutes packing the sail in the canvas bag and lacing it up again. The head of the sail has to be lashed down close to the deck and the halliard is taken up because if it is loose it will get caught behind the spreaders. I check that there are no stray ends on the foredeck and go aft to take up the slack on the sheets before retrimming the self-steering to cope with the slightly different trim of the ship under these sails.

All this has taken just over an hour, but the boat feels more comfortable and it is still sailing at over seven knots. To date I have made sixteen sail changes and there will be more before the end of the race. Every one leaves me drained of energy; less for the effort involved than for the fear of falling overboard or having a sail jam aloft. I decide against setting the number two jib. After every sail change there is a feeling of release and a sense of achievement and to-day, as usual, I have a twenty-minute nap by way of reward.

I woke up feeling much better and started to cook a dinner of soup, steak and steamed pudding. During the night the wind reached Force 7 and swung around to the south-south-west. Before daylight I set the number two jib because the boat could take more sail with the wind abeam.

Saturday, June 8th

The eighth was a day of powerful sailing and by six o'clock the speedometer was pointing to ten and a half knots with the sky promising more wind to come. After the cold northerly breezes of the past six days it was a welcome change to feel the balmy south wind on my face as I sat and watched *Lipton* tearing through the long and regular sea. There had been so much beating during the last week that I had been able to hold *Lipton* on the Great Circle course for a total of only fifty-five miles out of one thousand one hundred in distance run. Now I was steaming towards Newport at a spanking rate, but the English

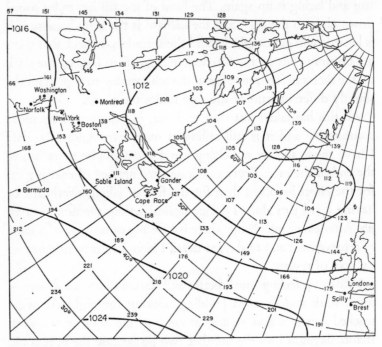

IIA *Barometric Pressure Map III*

The isobars are more closely spaced on Map IV (1968) than on Map III in the North Atlantic for the first half of June 1968.

Electric course prediction suggested I sailed north of the Great Circle route in order to hold the beam winds for longer.

The English Electric course prediction had been favouring reaching courses to a greater extent than I thought was justified, and I pulled out the graphs of the vessel's performance which had been fed into the computer. I remembered that I had given the reaching sector of the polar graph a more positive value than it deserved in the hope that this would make the computer search for the beam winds. It was doing this, but the greater speed on a reach was not enough to offset the increase in distance, and for

88

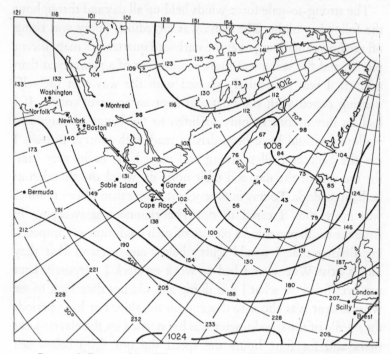

IIB. *Barometric Pressure Map IV*

(1951– 66). This means that there were stronger than average winds

the rest of the race I amended the instructions I was sent from Bayswater to allow for this bias. During the morning message from English Electric, Dick Moore told me that they had found something wrong with the distance to Newport calculation. Apparently the formula for finding the distance between two points on the globe, which had been taken from a well-known textbook on navigation, was quite wrong, and Ian Slater spent four hours on Friday night solving the problem from the first principles of spherical trigonometry! This morning's calculations were much more realistic.

The strong-to-gale force winds held up all day and throughout the following night. The noise was incredible. Spray was rising off the bows and flying over the starboard quarter in a magnificent plume, and the wake was more reminiscent of a powerboat than a ketch. I was particularly pleased with the way that the self-steering coped with the boat and kept an accurate course. If I had sat down content only to listen to the bangs, thumps and wallops I would have been driven mad with worry. Instead, I ran the generator all morning and played the radio very loud for the rest of the day and their noise drowned the thunderous bedlam on deck. To stay in the cockpit longer than fifteen minutes was more than I cared to do. The chaotic seas sweeping in from the south presented a picture of such confusion and impending disaster that I would scurry below and pretend that they didn't exist. Whenever I had to work on deck I purposely kept my eyes fixed on what I was doing and did not dare look to see what horror was about to descend on the ship. For long periods the needle of the speedometer was hypnotised by the eleven-knot mark and for four hours the speed did not drop below ten knots. Four times during the day the rotators of the log which protruded through the hull were swept away and I used up all my spares. Twice I crawled up into the bows to see if there was any movement of the hull walls when the boat was shaken by the explosion of bursting on to a wave, and although the shock travelled right through the ship I could feel no panting in the glassfibre laminate. During the twenty-four hours following 11 a.m. on Saturday, *Lipton* sailed two hundred and eleven miles and this is still her longest day's run. It was a glorious, thrilling sail, but I was not sorry for the wind to die down and allow peace to return.

9

Mid-Atlantic

Sunday was a dull day. It started well enough when Robert Clark's voice came over the radio telephone on my early morning call to David Thorpe. We discussed various aspects of handling the boat and I was pleased to catch a note of guarded optimism in his voice. An hour later the fog rolled in and reduced the visibility to fifty yards. Curiously, I found the fog very comforting. For once I was given a visible wall to my limitless world, and I liked this feeling of being contained in a small space. Yet another day of beating in twenty to twenty-five-knot winds, and although the seas were not much calmer the fog wisely hid them from me. The sun cleared the fog for a few hours in the middle of the day and I had a chance to get a noon sight and an afternoon sight. This more or less confirmed my dead reckoning position, but it did seem that I was not allowing enough for the North Atlantic Drift, which was pushing me back as much as fifteen miles per day. The wind was blowing from the south-west, and late in the afternoon the barometer started to fall.

My eating habits verged on the ridiculous. The only other time I had existed for a long period without a normal diet was on the expedition to Persia. I well remember becoming addicted to Ryvita, Cooper's Oxford Marmalade and tins of steak and kidney pie. If it had been possible I would have eaten these three items in dutiful rote for three months, and joyfully excluded the exciting possibilities in our trunks of food. I expected my eating habits to follow the same compulsive pattern on the race although I was well aware of the danger of not getting a proper diet. For the latter I relied on my plundered boxes. The food in these was excellent, quick and easy to prepare and with so much variety that it was like opening a Christmas stocking every day of the week. First of all I sorted out the dried meat, dried greens and dried fruit and put them aside with the proviso that I would supplement them with a real dinner of the same content, but cooked with conventional foods. It was in my arrangements for the substitute meals that my addictions ran riot. The difficulty was I would not know what I wanted to eat until I was at sea. I expected the race to last twenty-one days so I loaded a whole series of evening meals in twenty-one day lots. In fact my addiction showed itself on the first night of the race with steak and steamed pudding. The steaks ran out after eight days, and for the remainder of the race my dinners regularly consisted of chicken, noodles and steamed pudding. On Sunday night I was weaning myself off steaks and transferring to chicken.

Monday, June 10th

The worst thing about the second week at sea was that both Dick Moore and David Thorpe were unable to take my calls. Now the people detailed to stand in for them were quite excellent in every way, but because I knew both David and Dick and did not know their substitutes, I did not look forward so eagerly to the radio transmissions. I was now well beyond the range of the two megacycle station at Land's End and was using eight megacycles and calling Baldock. Here there was change of procedure, because it was no longer necessary to switch to working frequencies once contact had been made. Instead, *Lipton* had a reserved period of two half-hour periods per day on pre-arranged frequencies, and I called Baldock and had my conversation without switching over. The G.P.O. radio operators at Baldock must take much of the credit for our trouble-free radio communication. They were absolutely tireless in switching aerials around to help transmission, they always listened for me when I called and always had a word of encouragement at the end of the conversation. In many cases it was easier to call from mid-Atlantic than it was to make a trunk call at home, and it was always more reliable than calling from a 'phone box!

A news flash on the light programme at half past nine said that *Voortrekker* and *Raph* were in the lead. Immediately my spirits sank to their lowest ebb and I took out my vengeance on the boat. The barometer was still falling and the anemometer showed twenty-eight knots as *Lipton* ploughed to windward at an incredible eight knots. I was puzzled that on previous days in the same conditions the boat had seemed to sail slower. The wind was north-west, and I was so furious to think that I had fallen back that I was determined to drive the boat as it had never been driven before. I asked English Electric at eleven o'clock to check on the news report and they replied that this information appeared to be quite bogus and had not been put out by the race committee. Although it was hard going for *Lipton* all day, it was much worse for the competitors to the south. The advice of the long-range weather forecast had paid off and I had sailed north of the deep depression which so worried the other boats.

Towards noon the skies cleared momentarily and I managed to get a sight. Or rather, I managed to get a series of five sights which were then plotted on graph paper and an average of the best sights was taken as the result. Halfway through the afternoon I took a crawl and scramble around the deck to check on all the gear. It was still blowing at twenty-eight knots as I stretched over the tiller and pulled myself up to windward on the upper

Length overall	53·16′ (16·1 m.)	Length waterline	38·75′	(11·8 m.)
Beam	13·08′ (4 m.)	Draft	7·33′	(2·24 m.)
Displacement	15·0 tons	Sail area	1360 sq. ft.	(126·7 sq. m.)

Owner: Lt. Leslie Williams. *Designer*: E. G. van de Stadt. *Builders*: Tyler Boat Co., Southern Ocean Supplies and Lt. Leslie Williams

12A. *Spirit of Cutty Sark*: Sail plan

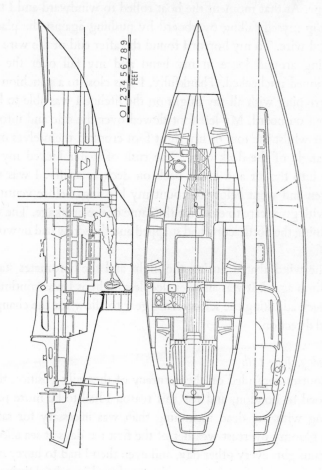

12B. *Spirit of Cutty Sark:* Arrangement

Ease of handling does not depend on the size of the sails alone but rather on the ratio between the sail area and the stability of the working platform. Although the *Cutty Sark* has large working sails these would have been easier to handle had she been a stiff vessel, but with a ballast ratio over 20% below that of *Lipton's*, she was rather tender. Her balanced rudder needs very little helm to tack the boat. Both in the cockpit and saloon there was too much room for the singlehanded sailor to move with comfort.

95

lifeline. At that moment the boat rolled to windward and I tried to stop myself falling overboard by pushing against the plastic-coated wire. To my horror I found the after end of the wire was waving around loose in my hand and my fall over the side continued unchecked. Thankfully, I was close to a stanchion and by gripping with all my might on the lifeline I was able to hold myself on board. My left foot slewed over the side and into the water whilst the toes of my right foot crooked themselves on to the angle of the deck edge. The rush of water kicked my left foot into the air and I was back on deck in a jiffy. I was very shaken and went below to count my blessings before venturing aft with great care to examine the cause of the breakage. The wire retaining the bottlescrew had snapped and the screw had unwound itself.

The wind abated during the night and the barometer started to climb again. It was another sleepless night as I was continually on deck adjusting the self-steering gear to allow for the changing wind direction.

Tuesday, June 11th

Courses depended on the accuracy of the daily position that I radioed to London, and for this reason I had to be more pains-taking with my dead reckoning than was necessary for safety. The gloomy overcast weather of the first ten days at sea allowed me sunsights every other day, and even then I had to hurry up to catch the sun before it was again enveloped in mist. During the afternoon I fell to fiddling with the radio transmitter and tuned the receiver to the current frequency for calling Baldock. To my surprise I heard Bruce Dalling on *Voortrekker*. He was having difficulty in making himself heard at Baldock, and when the transmission was over I warmed up my transmitter and started to call Baldock on the same frequency. I knew that Bruce had booked a half-hour call and there was a ten-minute gap before the next traffic was due. I called for eight or nine minutes, but could not raise the radio station. I was encouraged by this because it might mean that I was out of range at that particular time of the day and was therefore farther west than *Voortrekker*. I knew that a dozen other factors were involved and I purposely chose to ignore these!

Just before sunset, when I was tidying up on deck, I sighted up the mainmast and was stunned to find it bending sideways. I tore the insulating tape off the rigging screws. These had been screwed down as far as they could go and there seemed to be no hope of taking up the stretch in the rigging. As usual in times of crisis I went aft to sit in the cockpit and decide what to do. It was already getting dark so I put off action until the morrow. The prospect of losing my mast nine hundred miles from land made my mouth go dry.

Tuesday night was hard work. The wind continued to change direction every forty minutes or so and I was frequently on deck. I was worried about the mast and slept for less than three hours during the twenty-four.

Wednesday, June 12th

It was still dark when I sent my early morning radio transmission to *The Daily Telegraph*. I kept my clocks on Greenwich Mean Time so the farther west I sailed the earlier was my transmission. Conditions are generally better at night, so the change in time compensated for the greater distance that the radio waves had to travel. This morning I woke up just before transmission time and did not have long enough to prepare my log and notes. In my hurry I noted down the latitude and longitude of a cross on the chart which marked a Great Circle point and not my dead reckoning position.

Wednesday dawned bright and clear. The wind decided to blow from the north-west and brought with it high cumulus clouds and a bright sun for the first time in the race. This was a Treleigh cemetery sky which heightened the sense of crisis and deepened my fears about the mast. Four hours later a blast from a ship's siren had me on deck in a flash to find the Dutch vessel *Statendam* crossing my bows. Passengers and crew lined the rails to wave and the ship gave three more blasts on its siren. I was mildly annoyed at being disturbed and jealous of the passengers who were probably enjoying breakfast in great comfort. The liner circled around upwind of me and started to drift down towards the boat while my sails were shielded from the wind by the liner's wall-like sides. I gybed and ran off before my giant suitor who, in a fit of jealousy, steamed around in a big circle to wait for me downwind. I hauled my sheets in, reset the self-steering and headed off to the west at eight knots.

Down below I switched on the radio transmitter and bobbed back on deck to keep a watch on the ship. When the radio had warmed up I started calling *Statendam* on the ship-to-ship frequency. I intended to thank the Captain for his interest, tell the radio officer that all was O.K., would they please report my position to Lloyd's and kindly go away because they were making me very anxious. I could not get through, but *Statendam* got the message from my last manoeuvre, flipped her tail and resumed her course. She did report my position and immediately brought my navigational error to everyone's notice. I had already spotted my mistake, but it was too late to stop the journalists claiming that I was either a rotten navigator or that I was deviously plotting to fox the opposition. The truth of the matter was that I overslept.

At about midday the wind dropped from twenty to twelve knots and I set about the rigging screws. I carried two enormous wrenches which weighed about twenty pounds apiece and were over three feet long. I clamped one of these to the shroud terminal and another to the barrel of the screw and pulled with all my might. To my surprise they started to screw up. Obviously there was some thread that I could not see. I screwed up the other two bottle screws, tacked the boat and tightened the new leeward side. Then I went forward and checked the forestays. After four hours hard work and with water continuously swishing up my trouser legs I had straightened the mast and rid myself of this worry. The high, bright Treleigh sky acknowledged defeat and the wind went round to the south-west bringing with it my beloved sea mist.

The radio receiver was the best indicator of my progress. It hinted that I was getting towards the Canadian shore. It could no longer pick up the Light programme, but Canadian radio stations were booming in loud and clear.

I don't remember Wednesday night.

Thursday, June 13th

Thursday was an 'off day'. Wednesday had been an 'on day'. During 'on days' I felt full of vigour and set to work on the daily cleaning, checking and tightening chores with a will. I was glad to hear the clatter of the generator. I scorned my books and my berth and generally fussed around the boat like an old woman. On 'off days' it would be a great effort to get out of my berth. I would put off all those jobs which were not urgent and spent my time reading in my berth instead of sitting at the chart table and urging *Sir Thomas* to greater efforts. 'On days' and 'off days' seem to follow no set pattern and I spent hours trying to find the cause of them. I changed my diet, stopped drinking, fiddled with the ventilation, took off wet clothes and put on dry clothes, took off dirty dry clothes and put on damp clean clothes and still

I couldn't fathom the reason. This obscure pattern had overlays whose causes were easy to decipher.

My over-riding concern was my position in the race. For the past week there had been no definite news of *Raph* and *Cheers*, although I was comfortably ahead of *Spirit of Cutty Sark* and *Golden Cockerell*. I was continually analysing the weather and trying to work out how these conditions would be affecting the other boats. My spirits seesawed as I pieced together the scanty facts in different combinations which put me a hundred miles ahead, then a hundred astern of my illusory competitors. But over the past few days I was ahead more often than I was astern, largely because *Lipton* had not been stopped by any gear failures. By concentrating on the memory of fast sailing I became increasingly fanatic about sailing the boat as quickly as it would go. If I relaxed once I knew that this drive would tumble like a pack of cards. Just after ten the wind died away and left *Lipton* lifeless. English Electric had told me to expect this lull, but it would be followed by a fifteen-knot breeze from the north-west. Up on the foredeck I dropped the number two jib in a heap and ran up number one. Without the Brookes and Gatehouse instruments I am sure I would have said to myself, 'Becalmed, nothing I can do, better go below and rest.' But the anemometer showed that there was a two-knot wind, and the apparent wind direction indicator said it was coming from the west-south-west. With this encouragement I spent an hour trimming the sails trying to coax the boat forward. *Lipton* was travelling too slowly for it to register on the log and I could only guess at our progress by spitting in the water and watching my saliva drift astern. I steered towards a foggy north-west.

This was the first time for ten days that I had to steer by hand, the first time that there was not enough wind to swing the vane, the first time that the ship had been quiet except for the gentle swish of the servo blade as it dragged through the water. How I loved the peaceful solitude. Francis Chichester was right when he said the North Atlantic was full of spirits. I had a definite feeling that people had been here before. Some of them had perished; and was it their ghosts which seemed to dance at the very limit of my vision? One moment they would be in the fog and as I turned my head I felt that they just came into sight, but by the time I looked back at that spot on the smoky, grey wall that circled the boat they would have disappeared.

I brought my lunch of raisins, fruit bars and soup into the cockpit and left the cabin to dry out. I had designed the fore hatches badly, and as soon as any water splashed on to the foredeck it would drip down into the bilges. Mistake number two was forgetting to provide a sump for the bilge water, and consequently before there was enough water to bale into a bucket or to be sucked up by the bilge pump it would be running up the side of the hull and splashing over my bunk. The blankets and mattress varied between damp and wet for the whole trip, and to-day's calm gave my inefficient paraffin stove a chance to dry them. I lived in my oilskin trousers so the damp bed did not worry me very much.

Apart from the ship and the occasional radio programme there was nothing to distract my mind from worrying about my position in the race and from being acutely aware of how I felt. In this laboratory for the introverted mind, the effect of food and sleep on my morale was very marked. Surprisingly, alcohol usually failed to dispel my depression, whereas raisins and glucose acted like a shot in the arm.

Just after three o'clock, catspaws started walking across the water. I greeted them with mixed feelings. It would mean that *Lipton* would pick up his heels and start to run through the water again. It also meant the end of my peaceful interlude and this made me sad. As the wind got progressively stronger I began to wonder if it would go on and on, blowing harder and harder until it reached hurricane force; but it levelled off at fifteen knots. Enough to make me drop number one and run up number two.

That evening I listened on Radio St. John (Newfoundland) to the weather forecast for the Grand Banks. Since English Electric were supplying me with a private forecast I had not bothered to listen to *The Observer* forecast before. Tonight I tuned in. Baldock started broadcasting at eight o'clock: 'This is London calling, this is London calling, this is London calling, this is London calling. Here is the special weather forecast for competitors in the singlehanded transatlantic race. Storm warning . . . storm Force 10 is expected in sea area . . . .' I snapped the receiver off. The funereal tones of the broadcaster were exactly like those I had heard at the announcement of the death of King George VI and I didn't want to be depressed by news of Force 10 in an area which didn't affect me because I was sure that my devious imagination would find a reason why it should come my way before the night was out.

10

Fog, Ice and Reflections

On Thursday night I stayed awake as long as I could before taking a nap. It must have been three-thirty before I turned in. There was a period of an hour and a half each day when I found it practically impossible to stay awake. This period moved forward with the sun as I sailed farther west and always seemed to start about three hours before dawn. I slept for an hour and a half before being roused by the off-course alarm and the alarm clock ringing simultaneously.

Friday, June 14th

I did not have a relaxed sleep for the entire race, and this morning's rest must have been deeper than usual because I woke up with the feeling that I hadn't been aware of what was going on for the past hour or so. Immediately I knew that something was wrong. I was lying on my stomach, but my stomach was facing the back wall of the bunk instead of the seat because *Lipton* was heeling so much. It was pitch dark and the noise was appalling. I lay in my blue blanket for a few moments hoping that it was a dream and that I would really wake up to find that everything was all right. But I was awake and something would have to be done unless I wanted to blow out my sails or lose my mast. I reached up to pull the compass on to its side and saw that we were thirty-five degrees off course. A low-pitched whine from the magnetic log told me that the hammering of the bows on the waves had again broken off the rotators. Behind me there was a crash and the chart table swung on to its side as the pin which is used to change the angle of the table was shaken out of its hole. The off-course alarm stopped ringing. The water in the bilges was deeper than I remembered seeing it.

It took me a few minutes to collect my senses and I started to loathe the task ahead. I threw my blue blanket on to the top berth, sat up and pulled on my seaboots. Pictures of being swept off the deck by a wave, of the mast going over the side and of losing the boom and sail overboard all raced through my mind in horrid confusion.

Boots on, now the top, towel round my neck, button up my jacket and tie it around my waist. Safety harness on for the first time. The boat is crashing from one wave to the next with a terrible velocity. Speed—nine knots, close reaching, anemometer thirty-five to forty knots—whole gale. Moving from hand-hold to hand-hold I worm my way aft and stick my head through the hatch. It's raining, or is that spray? Thank God it's night—I don't want to see those waves! Some halliards are trailing in the sea and water is sweeping along the starboard side in an unbroken torrent. I reach in for the switch box and put on the forepeak lights and cabin light. These shine through the transparent fore-hatches and the perspex dome to give me light on deck. I move up the windward side and slide down to the mast. The steel pulpit on the leeward side of the mast is continually immersed in water and *Lipton* is heeling sickeningly. I snap my safety harness to the mast, wrap my legs around the pulpit and free the tail of the main halliard. When this is ready to run I slip the halliard off the winch and let it slide against the barrel. As the boom drops, its outer end catches in the mizzen forestay and the sail tumbles on to the deck but is soon washed over the side. It takes me half an hour to wrap the sail on to the boom and strap the whole lot on to the deck. I have to keep both arms wrapped around the boom to stop myself being swept overboard, and as I have to work lying flat on the deck it feels as if I am swimming in a shallow stream.

By the time the deck is tidy I am soaked to the skin. *Lipton* feels easier and the wind is not quite so strong. I watch the boat from the cockpit, decide against taking the mizzen down and go below to choose the least wet towel for drying myself. It is five-thirty. No more sleep tonight, so I sit at the chart table to think, and wait, and watch the miles go by.

It is still dark when I make my early morning radio call to London. I am already on the fringe of the ice area and am worried because I have heard no ice reports on the special broadcast for the race competitors. I ask the *Telegraph* to find out when these broadcasts are going to start and, in a tired voice, I relay my daily data. After the broadcast I go on sitting at the chart table and the next thing I know is waking up with my head on the charts.

Friday has dawned to throw light on the chaos of the cabin. It is not a pretty sight. Food has fallen out of one of the lockers and a teabag has burst open and the bilge water is busy stirring up a cold, salt brew of Lipton's worst. Some of my blankets have fallen down behind my berth and are soaking wet. A chart has slipped off the table. There are a good two hours' pumping and baling to do before the bilges are reasonably dry, and I decide to finish this before breakfast. When this is done it is already time for my second radio transmission. It does nothing to raise my spirits because the forecast is for another day of twenty to twenty-five knot winds from the south-west.

By noon the wind has lightened enough for the working rig, and it takes me an hour and a half to hoist the mainsail and tidy up on deck. The slamming is still severe and lasts all afternoon.

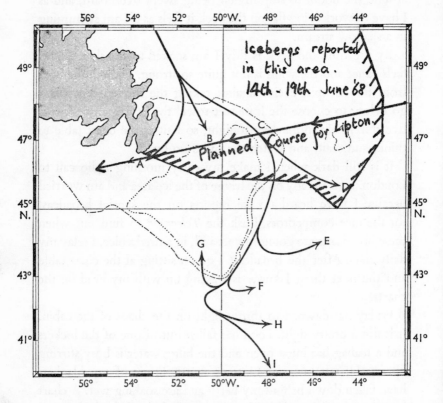

13. Chart to show limit of iceberg area, 14-19 June, 1968.

Figure 13 shows the predicted extent of the sea areas where icebergs and growlers can be expected during the month of June. I intended to cut a 150-mile passage through the corridor north of the wide, kidney-shaped area where the icebergs spread out to die. But during the afternoon I picked up an ice report from a Canadian radio station which gave a much wider ice limit than I had expected. I should be in the ice area before midnight. The

17A. *Pen Duick IV:* an intensely interesting boat which has since crossed the Atlantic with the trade winds in eleven days, an average of 280 miles per day, with a crew of three.

17B. Eric Tabarly.

18. *Raph:* if I had been faced by a facsimile of
Lipton I would have been very worried indeed
and I respected *Raph* most of all because her
pedigree was closest to my steed's,

19. The Gianoli self-steering gear on *Raph*.

20. *Voortrekker:* although *Voortrekker*'s waterline length is only 2·5 less feet than *Sir Thomas Lipton*'s, her displacement is only half as much. Bruce Dalling logged the second longest day's run on the race: 225 miles.

fog closed in during the afternoon and visibility was down to less than a cable. It is unusual to have fog and a strong wind in the English Channel but it seems commonplace on the Banks. Statistically one's chances of avoiding an iceberg are only marginally improved by keeping a sporadic watch, so I fill a sailbag with dry clothes, some emergency rations and a bottle of gin, haul my life raft into the cockpit and retire below.

Although radio communication with Baldock was still excellent I was wondering if I was close enough to the American shore to contact WOO, Ocean Gate—a radio station near New York. After half an hour's rummaging in the radio handbooks I found that the crystal fitted to my radio is only used by WOO during the winter months, and twenty minutes of calling failed to raise them.

Before dinner I switched on the Loran set and let it warm up for a few minutes. I should be close enough to pick up ground wave signals from Newfoundland. After half an hour's fiddling with the dials I was tolerably satisfied with two signals and transferred their position lines to the Admiralty charts. They agreed with my dead reckoning position and suggested that I was using the right technique on the Loran set. It is difficult to plot the Loran lines of position on an Admiralty chart and I decided to transfer my dead reckoning to the multicoloured Loran charts.

I had an early dinner and turned in about midnight. An hour later I woke up with a start and rushed over to the chart table. Everything seemed all right, then I noticed the log. I was in the ice area. I peeped through my dome half expecting to see acres of pack ice rising across my track, but in the fog I could see no farther than the stem of the boat. *Lipton* was nosing inquisitively through the gloom.

I managed two and a half hour's sleep during the night and

spent the remaining hours listening to the sound of water slipping past the hull. I hoped that the boat's speed did not fall off so much that I would have to hoist the number one in the dark. Happily the speedometer did not drop below the point where my conscience would have me pulling on my oilskin jacket and top boots.

Saturday, June 15th

Saturday turned out to be a bad, bad day. Daylight chased the wind away and by nine o'clock *Lipton* was rolling around in the swell and punching all the shape out of the boomed sails. I spent an hour trying to prevent the booms from rushing to and fro with each roll of the ship, was defeated and dropped them all on deck in disgust. I slipped down through the forehatch and pulled up the ghoster, snapped the piston hanks on the stay and ran it to the masthead. I ambled aft, sheeted the sail and hoisted the mizzen staysail. These set better than the boomed sails, but within an hour they too were hanging limp.

The wind seemed to come from the direction that English Electric predicted. It was so slow that only my anemometer could pick up the zephyrs of one knot. The fog cleared sufficiently for me to get some sunsights and I retired to my chart table to plot them on a graph, work out the result, plot it on the chart, bring up the morning's line of position, take a series of Loran lines of position and compare these with the sunsights. To my surprise all six lines crossed in a small hexagon no more than a sixteenth of an inch across. From now on I would rely more and more on the Loran, checking it against radio beacons, depth soundings and Nantucket consolan. It was much quicker than taking sunsights, and more convenient when the sun only appeared for a few minutes each day.

If one gets it into one's head that all the other competitors are without wind then being becalmed can be very pleasant. But today I was sure that I was in the eye of a low and that all the other boats were steaming along at a rate of knots. I paced around the deck in a state of considerable neurosis and busied myself with a host of odd jobs. The number one jib had torn itself against a spreader and this took over an hour to patch. I ran the cabin heater to dry out some clothes and listened to all the weather reports on the Canadian shore to try to work out when and from where the wind would be coming. These endorsed the English Electric forecast but added that a tropical storm Brenda was reported south of Bermuda moving east. I dragged out my gnomonic chart and plotted its position. If it kept going east that would be all right. If it turned north then we could be in its path.

Lipton was becalmed for nineteen hours and at the next transmission time I was only forty-three miles closer to Newport. The worst day so far and it turned out to be the worst day of the race. The only consolation was that I ran no risk of damaging my boat on an iceberg at this speed.

Saturday's calm marked the end of the Atlantic section of the voyage. Up until then I had had almost continuous headwinds between Force 3 and Force 6 which made the going very hard on the boat. Although it was uncomfortable for me there had been only two or three sail changes per day, and it had mainly been a question of holding one's breath and hoping that nothing would break.

Sunday, June 16th

On Sunday I remarked that the first two weeks of the race had offered typical Atlantic weather and this might appear to be a precocious remark coming from someone who was venturing beyond the Western Approaches for the first time. My reading and Robert's advice had so accurately forecast the conditions I had met on the voyage that already I was feeling like an old hand at transatlantic sailing.

I had reached the Grand Banks lean, fit and hungry for faster sailing, for although I had driven the boat hard it was always about five per cent below the limit. I was very aware of the pickle I would be in if I lost my mast in mid-Atlantic. Now that I was within striking distance of Newfoundland but not so close that I need worry about running aground, my attitude towards the race changed and I decided to throw all caution to the winds in trying to squeeze the utmost out of *Sir Thomas*. For the first time I measured the distance to Newport on the chart and I started to think in terms of distance to go to the finish rather than the number of miles come from Plymouth. I felt that the Atlantic was as good as crossed, and whereas I had been enjoying myself in a painful sort of way until this morning, now the pain started to slip away.

I told David Thorpe that *Sir Thomas* had been running very quickly and now he was sprinting. After my second call to English Electric, Baldock asked me to hold because there was more traffic for me. I wondered who on earth could be calling and feared some disaster had befallen my parents. Eventually, a Mr. Fraser of *The Sun* asked if he could interview me for his newspaper. I was amazed that anyone had managed to get through to me and would like to have answered all his questions. I still had a contract with *The Daily Telegraph* and decided to give him only my longitude and latitude. I felt rather like a captured soldier giving his name, rank and number but refusing to answer further questions.

A brisk north-west wind brought a sparkling sky and temperatures in the upper thirties. I climbed the rigging to look for icebergs but I could see no glinting reflections. The day passed happily and without incident. I slept for three hours and continued to throw my imagination into the desert by reading T. E. Lawrence's *The Seven Pillars of Wisdom*. It was more and more difficult to stay awake for my first radio transmission at 6 a.m., but I was always amused to hear Baldock wake David Thorpe. I could hear the operator say that the yacht *Sir Thomas Lipton* was calling David Thorpe and could he take the call? David would sound faint and half asleep, but by the time the operator had asked me to go ahead David would be bouncing with energy and enthusiasm. Every morning he was full of encouragement and I looked forward to talking to him.

Monday, June 17th

Before the last war celestial navigation was, with some justification, a subject for experts who had had a formal training. Now that the sight reduction tables have been simplified there is no reason why any slightly intelligent person should not grasp the principles of yacht navigation and put them into operation with the greatest confidence. It is not difficult, it is not mathematics, it is purely a question of remembering a few simple ideas, being careful and putting in some practice. In ordinary passage-making and ocean-voyaging there is no black magic, nothing complicated and no need for a God-given ability to succeed as a navigator. There are, however, two occasions when people who have a flair for the subject will have an advantage over the others. The first of these is when the navigator has to weigh up a mass of contradictory data and choose the most reliable information to fix his position. The second is in trying to evaluate forecasts of current, weather and boat speed in choosing the fastest route. This is where the computer had been an invaluable companion during the race, and in figures 14A

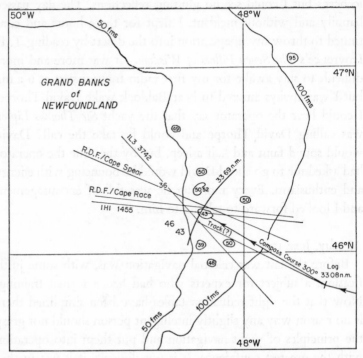

Map labels:
- 50°W
- 48°W
- 47°N
- 46°N
- 50 fms
- 100 fms
- 100 fms
- 50 fms
- 100 fms
- GRAND BANKS of NEWFOUNDLAND
- 95
- 49
- 50
- 50 52
- 50
- 43
- 39
- 48
- 50
- IL3 3742
- R.D.F./Cape Spear
- R.D.F./Cape Race
- IHI 1455
- 36
- 46
- 43
- Track (?)
- 33 69 n.m.
- Compass Course 300°
- Log 3308 n.m.
- 48°W

14A. *Position Finding on Edge of Grand Banks, 17th June. 12.00 hrs.*
Dead reckoning position is on arc 3369 but there is an unknown set to the
south by the Labrador current. Depth sounder gives 43 fms. but is this on
the Grand Banks or the 43 fm. submarine plateau? Thick fog makes sun sight
impossible therefore take two Loran lines of position and two bearings on
the R.D.F. stations on Cape Race and Cape Spear. These confirm position
on 43 fm. submarine plateau.

14B. (See next page) *Tactical Navigation on Edge of Grand Banks. 17th June.*
Given. Position at Log 3379 n.m./1425 hours. Series of Loran lines of position
show current setting to the south at $\frac{1}{2}$ knot. Pilot chart shows Labrador current
setting towards WSW on Banks but S on edge of Banks. True wind speed—
5 knots, direction SSW. Weather forecast: Wind light and variable, mostly
south, veering to northwest at 15 knots late today.
Choice of courses. English Electric Choice No. 1.
                     English Electric Choice No. 2.
                         Great Circle Course (see chart)
Course sailed. English Electric Choice No. 1.

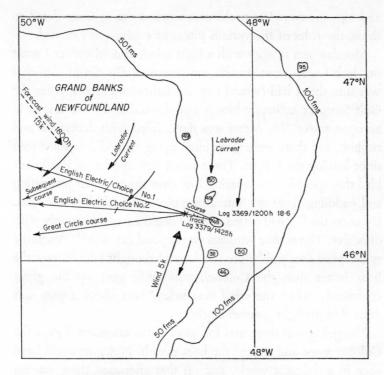

Reasons. Boat speed English Electric Choice No. 1—5·7 knots.

         Boat speed English Electric Choice No. 2—5·4 knots.

         Boat speed Great Circle Course—5·2 knots.

These values obtained from graphs of boat's performance (see Figure 5, p. 60). Percentage increase in speed of Choice No. 1 over Great Circle course is 9% but increase in distance sailed is only 6%. Therefore choice No. 1 justified. (Relative distances worked out on chart.)

Additional factors

(a) Choice No. 1 course will carry *Lipton* to stronger NW winds more quickly than Great Circle course.

(b) 'Subsequent course' has a favourable slant relative to NW wind.

(c) Labrador current will help to sweep track of *Lipton* closer to Great Circle course while boat exploits faster point of sailing.

(d) This course carried *Lipton* to more favourable WSW current by shortest route.

Result. NW wind set in at 20·15 hrs., speed 14 knots. *Lipton* tacked and followed 'subsequent course'!

and 14B the complete problem is worked out in some detail to show the roles of the various pieces of equipment I carried.

Monday was muggy with a light wind, and whenever I went on deck I was covered with condensation. By eleven o'clock I was sure that I had crossed into the Labrador current. After the Gulf Stream's antiseptic blue it now looked as if I was sailing in an open sewer. The water was dark, filled with driftwood and rubbish, and there were more birds flying around than I had seen since leaving the Scillies. There was a new species—a small dark bird that spent its time soaring low over the water or just sitting and paddling from one interesting piece of rubbish to the next. By noon the fog had closed in and I could see my mast only with difficulty. The anchor windlass was beyond my world. When the wind speed dropped below five knots I thought I could steer the boat better than the Colonel, who only gave up the ghost completely when the wind was below two knots. *Lipton* was dressed in his light weather clothes.

The going was slow, and for most of the afternoon I gave the Colonel a rest and steered the boat myself. Newport could have been in a different world, and on that afternoon there was no nagging desire to reach its harbour. Towards evening a great calm spread across the sea and entered my mind. I had found peace with myself.

Lipton still had steerage way and I reckoned he would pass on to the submarine plateau of the Banks just after seven o'clock. At about a quarter to eight the needle of the depth sounder started to flicker away from its permanent home against the stop and within ten minutes was pointing confidently to forty-five fathoms. Another series of Loran lines of position showed the current to be in my favour although setting slightly to the south. My tactical prognostications had borne fruit. I was happy. It was dark so I turned off all the lights in the cabin and lay down with

21. Bill Howell capsized *Golden Cockerel* in 1967 and I thought that the memory of this would stop him driving the boat to the limit.

22. *Spirit of Cutty Sark*: of all the skippers in the race I thought that Les Williams would be the hardest man to beat,

my eyes shut. After twenty minutes I opened them and went on deck to find that I could see tolerably well.

Lipton was chuntering along at four and a half knots and the wind speed was only seven knots. We were sailing into a north-westerly wind. 'Beating to windward' would be too harsh an expression to describe this gentle sucking of *Lipton* towards Newport. The boat was heeling four degrees, Bruce Banks's sails were a delight to behold, and all the world was silent with a magic heaviness. I was no longer *Lipton's* helmsman. I became part of the ship. I was a limb of *Lipton*, another boom, another sail, another tiller; the ship and I were one. But *Lipton* was part of the scene so I became part of the scene, no longer outside looking in, but inside looking out. I was part of the chorus, neither conductor nor spectator but singing as part of the environment.

My existentialist reverie did not last long, for as I became more accustomed to the dark I could see that the fog had respectfully retreated to the limit of my vision. I liked that. Some hidden complex in my soul liked the idea of feeling in command of all I surveyed, and I was immediately jerked out of the scene and into command again. Well, *Lipton* was doing what he was told and what I could see was so delightfully limited by my dutiful fog that this complex was amply satisfied and laid to rest. This was a time for looking back and for looking forward. I had never been so happy. This mental admission of pleasure brought a swift and guilty reaction because I had not entered the race with the idea of being happy. I had not entered the race because I liked sailing, because I am not sure that I do. There are other sports which have given me more animal satisfaction.

I remember rowing a pair with Neil Jackson during our 'finals' year. On winter afternoons we used to slip downstream from Oxford until we came to the reach by Lock Wood near Abingdon. At about four we turned around and started to pull back against the flood. The mist would rise like smoke off the river and hang there just three feet above the water and our heads sculptured an inverted furrow in the foggy ceiling. I could close my eyes and stroke the boat along while Neil rowed at bow and steered. When the boat ran well the sensuousness of the motion could transport me from the boat until it felt like floating on air. When I opened my eyes I watched, hypnotised, as the ruled line of our wake and the measured puddles left by our oars disappeared into the gloom. Cows watched from the dank river banks.

I remember snapping over a hurdle, striding to the next, finding it exactly in my stride pattern and snapping again until ten hurdles were crossed in perfect pattern. I remember launching a javelin into a soft headwind and watching it float that extra ten feet as it rode the wind like a glider. I remember swimming down a wave until I was on top of it, going faster and faster until the gradient of the falling water swept me along for forty yards with the rush of it tingling against my tummy. I can remember the rare thrill of making a break in a Rugby game and passing within inches of the outstretched arms of the defenders. But generally Rugby was a roast beef and Yorkshire pudding game compared with the champagne of rowing. I can remember planing in a Redwing dinghy. If a Rolls-Royce car could plane then surely it would copy the Redwing. I have not ski-ed and I have heard such reports of its excitement that I am purposely avoiding it lest I become obsessed with this sport which is, for people living in England, remarkably inconvenient.

All these sensations are more immediately satisfying than single-handed sailing. The race was a sort of forty days and forty nights to be spent in the theatre of solitude, on a stage of discomfort and with props of fear and worry. Some eccentric streak whispered to my conscience that this catharsis would fortify my fortitude; that if some great and terrible crisis descended to find me not wanting then I would be the better for it. And here I was enjoying myself. It was rather like enjoying church. What a happy disappointment!

I wondered if the explorers of yesterday with their grand advertised aims of discovery were not sparked by the same eccentricities that lead increasing numbers to singlehanded sailing. For whereas our forefathers had goals left to aim at, these have all gone now and we have to be more naked in our desires and set up theoretical tasks in their stead. I wondered if they, too, having renounced all homely comforts for the rigours of the march, found a far greater, a far deeper pleasure from the utterly simple things in life than is possible in our sophisticated society. I could understand how the masochist concentrated on a painful thing until the total exclusion of everything else from his mind made that pain a delight! By severely restricting my environment the simple pastimes that remained became immensely pleasurable.

After working on *Lipton's* foredeck I used to feel tired. So I slept. My berth was damp and by any reasonable standards highly uncomfortable, but to me, with *Lipton* tramping on and looking after himself and when I was feeling satisfied after a good session of work on deck, my berth was more luxurious and comfortable than any bed I have known.

When I was hungry, I ate. In *Lipton* I explored the true taste of raisins, of porridge and of chocolate more thoroughly than I had ever done before or ever will again.

I was restricted in my walking space to fifty-seven feet of deck, but my sense of property was acute. The sky and sea dominated my mood, lifting me, carrying me, depressing me, frightening me, belittling me, beside their magnificence impressing upon me their implicit order and things beyond my ken.

The keynote is simplicity, and I remembered that the happiest I had been before this time was at Oxford where again one's horizons were truncated within a restricted enclave. Mountains and deserts, or rather the reasons why people have visited them, share with the sea the wide horizons and an essentially simple purpose. Some experiences in war and childhood seem to be distilled to the point of simplicity, but real life is complicated and I wondered if this abstract retreat was a good preparation for these complications. I think not, because people are needed. It was true that it gave me a marvellous perspective on life. I saw the people at home as if they had been stripped of all pretensions, for here there was only clear purpose, the real people and the important things in life. I was thinking more clearly and analytically than before, I was washing away the grit of an oddball; I was feeling more myself than I could ever have done without the race.

And as to the great and terrible crisis that was due to descend upon me . . . well, so far I had been spared. I didn't know that this was to come, but I well recognised the thrill of responding to it. When all of one's body is an unfeeling axe for the brain, when pain and tiredness slip away, when there is the deep satisfaction of knowing that this is exactly the way you wanted yourself to respond, when the simplicity of purpose fascinates and draws one like a moth to the lamp—all of this, coming in a few seconds of time which will live on for always as a great saga of contentment secret in one's heart . . . this is all very exciting. When this sweet has been tasted it can become an addiction so that one keeps returning to the precipice to look over and bask in the thrill of one's response to danger whether it be another bullfight, another mountain climb or another car race. And here lies the danger, for to repeat the process is merely to give vent to the bully in one's soul. I could not look at the sketches of my new boat for 1972 without a tinge of reproach. A second race, another go? Am I getting hooked? This was the very rejection of my motives for entering the race. One doesn't climb one's Everest twice. One moves on.

II

Sailing on a Plateau

Tuesday, June 18th

After Monday's soul-searching, Tuesday found me feeling full of work. At just after eleven o'clock the wind, as expected, filled in from the south-east. It was far enough aft to call for the running sails. Normally I would have cursed my luck and implored the wind to come round on the beam and spare me the labour of putting up the twins, but today I set to work with a spirit and had both sails pulling beautifully after an hour and a half. Before the sails were hoisted *Lipton* was doing four and a half knots in an apparent wind of five knots, but the twins gave the boat a lift and pushed her speed to over six knots. These sails seemed to be just as effective as a spinnaker.

It is when the wind falls light that the singlehander has most work to do. If he can move the boat a few miles he may well sail out of the windless zone and make up several hours sailing on a boat whose skipper relaxes and waits for the wind to come to him.

All day I had a strong sense of sailing in shallow water. I seemed able to sense the Grand Banks rising under my keel, and the fact that I was now in forty-four fathoms of water instead of four hundred and forty fathoms gave me a strange feeling of security. The shape of the waves seemed different from the open Atlantic and I had the impression that boats and people were near by. It is unusual to find icebergs on the Banks, so that worry was more or less over.

On Tuesday I must have got the most out of the boat with the least help from the wind. The anemometer did not rise above fourteen knots but *Lipton* ghosted a total of 157 nautical miles in twenty-four hours. *Thomas* was working so quietly and efficiently in his fog-bound circle of water and I was enjoying his motion so much that I did not want to go to bed.

Late that night I switched on the short-wave converter to check my chronometer. Instead of the usual pips and dashes of the time signal there was a whine of a police siren, the sound of traffic and people talking. It seemed that I was picking up the police radio from somewhere on the mainland. The nearest town of any size was over a hundred miles to the north. I spent an hour at my chart table plotting a series of Loran fixes. These showed that the Labrador current was at last beginning to sweep me towards the south-west. The wind was still blowing at twelve knots and the sea was flat. My course lay straight across the Virgin rocks where there is a depth of two fathoms, but as the wind was still light and there were no waves to drop me on to the rocks, I decided to go to bed and let *Lipton* sail on the same course.

Wednesday, June 19th

In an article that I drafted for *The Daily Telegraph* before the race I had described singlehanded sailing as a long spell in a prison hospital where you can earn remission of your sentence by frequent work-outs on a trampoline which is continually sprayed with very cold water. Early Wednesday was just like that. The wind hovered behind me, and my conscience forced me to work on the twins. After a couple of hours the wind finally decided to blow from the south-west, so down came the twins and up went the number two. By noon it was blowing at twenty knots and *Lipton* was on a collision course with Cape Race. Once more visibility was down to fifty yards and I was charging at eight and a half knots towards a rocky peninsula without having seen a landmark since leaving the Scillies seventeen days before. I kept a wary eye on my depth recorder while I had lunch. I wanted to stay on this tack because I expected the wind to go back to the south and give me a free passage past the headland. By the time I had finished my rice pudding I could bear the suspense of my very own brand of Russian roulette no longer and went on deck to put *Lipton* about. Just before dinner the sky cleared and for the first time in three days I could see for more than three hundred yards, and that stranger, the sun, burnt the moisture off my decks. I suppose I have always shunned the extrovert joys of summer—swimming, beaches and great gatherings of people in the open air which I would watch, secretly and at a distance. I have always preferred the quiet indoors and the retreat that fits the winter months, so I was not at all pleased to see the sun as it caught me unawares in my winter mind without having the manners to give me warning with a short spring. I had not washed since leaving Plymouth and I knew *Sir Thomas* was finding it difficult to live with me. Perhaps I ought to take a shower. Reluctantly I took my clothes off and religiously poured ten bucketfuls of icy water over myself. The shock was severe and I kept a strict count, longing for the release of the last shower and the feeling of well-being that floods the body after it has been doused.

Just before sundown two trawlers came drifting towards me from the horizon. They had a funny trick of dashing around in semi-circles, and when I got close I could see that they were from Russia. They paid no attention to their silent visitor as he ghosted by and they went on tending their nets with dull enthusiasm.

It blew up in the night and I had the mizzen down for a few hours. My log showed that I had run 2,711 miles through the water which is 200 miles short of the Great Circle distance from Plymouth to Newport. If this had been the 1964 race, with its higher percentage of beam winds and less beating, I would probably have been within 350 miles of Newport. As it was I had another 780 miles to go. One hundred and sixty miles today.

Thursday, June 20th

Now that I was within an area covered by frequent, detailed weather forecasts I began to rely less heavily on English Electric's work. Originally we had intended to finish their course predictions when I reached the Virgin rocks, but they had been so accurate and useful that I asked them to continue as far as Nantucket. The English Electric forecast had twice deflected me from the shortest course route to Newport and I had made a better days' run as a result. The most valuable help that the computer gave was the way it made the ship much more efficient. Practically every day I had information from the computer which tempered my decision about changing sails.

To change a jib on *Lipton* in a strong wind means going bareheaded for about forty minutes when changing down and the same when changing up. It can mean the loss of over two miles when compared with a sail change on a crewed boat. English Electric would often say that at 1800 hours the wind will rise to twenty-five knots from the south-south-west veering to the northwest at twelve knots for three hours then backing to the southwest at twenty knots. If I didn't know that this pattern of events was expected I would probably have made two sail changes and lost a couple of miles in the process.

On Thursday I was working the wind shifts as first one tack and then the other was the closer to the Nantucket Light Vessel. At this stage I was aiming at the Light Vessel, and my rumb line passed just north of Sable Island. I planned to give this hazard a wide berth and intended to take a long tack to the south so that I did not get boxed in between the island and the shore. I tacked forty-two times in fifteen hours that day, and it is such a simple operation that I did not notice the work. When I was off the best tack by fifteen degrees I went up into the cockpit, pulled the light nylon line to release the servo blades from the vane, pushed the tiller hard over and jammed a tiller line on a cleat. Then I whipped the handle out of the leeward winch and put it on the windward side, threw off the turns on the winch by which time the boat was coming through the eye of the wind. I had to release the tiller and start taking in on the new leeward side. Then I would trim the boat by hand until it was sailing at its fastest and drop the catch to engage the vane. I had become so confident with the vane gear that I never had to stay in the cockpit to see if it would work properly. I just knew it would.

Late in the afternoon the sky cleared and I brought up my sextant and notebook for a series of five sights. When I was on the third one a U.S. Navy aircraft showed up and began to circle the ship. After three circuits one of its propellers stopped turning and it limped off to the west. The appearance of this aircraft set me on edge because I had spent the last ten days not knowing where the other competitors were but imagining myself to be in the lead . . . tomorrow I would know the truth.

Just before dark the wind flitted around to the south and I hauled up the mizzen staysail. The weather forecast said that early next morning the wind would blow from the north-west at twenty eight knots. I decided to steer a little north of my present course so that when the wind went to the north-west I would be close enough to the shore to enjoy relatively calm water and a close reach.

Friday, June 21st

By 4 a.m. I reckoned that I had come far enough to the north, and as the wind was already beginning to veer towards the south-west it was high time I dropped the mizzen staysail. This was normally the easiest of sails to handle because all the work is around the cockpit in the protected part of the ship, and here the deck is at its widest to catch the sail as it comes down. There was no moon and it was very dark as I threw the turns off the halliard winch, but I could see that the last turn did not begin to run as the weight of the sail pulled on the halliard. 'Oh, my God,' I muttered aloud. The halliard had jammed aloft. Immediately I remembered that I had forgotten to change this wire halliard and it had jammed between the sheave and the cheek of the block. No amount of pulling would free it. It would only make matters worse. I broke out in a cold sweat as I realised that I would have to climb the mast and cut the sail down. I went below and sat at the galley table. Absent-mindedly I put my hand into the locker, felt for the glucose tin, pulled it out and started to mix a drink. To reach for the glucose tin was my first reaction in a crisis. *Lipton* was doing nine and a half knots and heeling about eight degrees which would put the top of the mizzen out above the sea. If I fell off when I was up there—that would be the end. I started to re-hearse the procedure and could think of no way in which a safety belt would either stop my fall, or prevent me from falling overboard. I never expected anything to go wrong on the mizzen and never considered putting steps on this mast, so now I would have to shin up the bare spar.

I pulled on my waterproof trousers because I thought these would grip the mast better than my woollen long-johns. The sea was moderately rough and *Lipton* was pitching. I climbed on to the mizzen halliard winch and ran my hand up the luff of the sail until it came to a slide. I grabbed this and wrapped my legs around the mast. Straightening my knees, I stretched for the tang of the jumper stay. As I was dragging my legs up again my trousers caught in the tang and stopped my upward thrust with a jolt. At the same time the boat pitched fiercely into a wave, sending a shudder through the mizzen and, finding me off balance, loosed me from the mast and threw me down on to the edge of the cockpit coaming. As I fell I collided with the halliard winch and I lay quiet for a few moments waiting for the shock of the fall to go away. I prayed that nothing was broken and gingerly moved my legs and arms to see if they still worked. Thankfully they did, but my right wrist was sprained and my left hand was bleeding. I was very shaken and went below to lie down and consider what to do next.

I decided to wait four hours until it was light. This would mean continuing in towards the Nova Scotian shore, but there was the promise of being able to drive out from the coast with a smart north-wester and slip between Sable Island and the mainland with a fair breeze. I checked this over in my mind before dragging myself to the chart table to see how far I could sail before reaching the shore. I reckoned I had six hours sailing on this course before having to turn south. Four hours would be taken up with waiting and there would be two hours of work to get the sail down. With this sail jammed aloft I could not tack because the main boom would catch on the sail. Nor could I go to windward effectively with 420 square feet of canvas flapping uselessly. I would just *have* to get that sail down in two hours or else I would put the whole boat in danger. I would be much happier about coming this far north if our course lay south of Nantucket instead of the Nantucket Light Vessel. I opened the chart table and pulled out the race instructions to check the course. To my surprise they read:

'. . . thence to Newport passing south of Nantucket.'

I turned to the Pilot and looked up Nantucket. The definition was a town on Nantucket Island. There was no mention of a light vessel. I was surprised because I could definitely remember Tabarly describing the Light Vessel in his book *Lonely Victory*, and I could not imagine why the race committee would change its mind. Although it would be a better route for me now that I had come so far north I thought that it would give the shallow draft multihulls an unfair advantage since they would be able to skirt the island itself while the deeper draft monohulls would have to go twenty miles further south. I cast my mind back to that noisy briefing exactly three weeks ago. No, I didn't remember Nantucket mentioned there and in any case we would be sure to have written amendments. I pulled out the chart for the Nantucket area and saw that the Light Vessel had been moved a few miles further south since 1964. This left a deep water passage between the shoals and the shipping lanes that use the Light Vessel as a homing beacon. I remembered that the Light Vessel had been demolished three times by ships, and reasoned that the committee had been very sensible to allow us to avoid these dense shipping lanes which are so often shrouded in fog. With these congratulations to the race committee I went back to my berth to wait for the dawn.

It was a very uncomfortable four hours. I didn't sleep but instead tried to work out other ways in which I could get the sail down. If I cut the luff at the foot of the sail perhaps I would be able to pull it off the luff wire. I thought that Bruce Banks had probably made a stouter job of it than this. Perhaps I could lash the sail to the mizzen mast. This was a very messy solution. The right thing to do was to climb the mast with my giant wire cutters and cut the halliard just below the block. Then I could use the topping lift as a mizzen halliard and the mizzen halliard for the staysail.

I lay in my bunk as all the world's earnest young men danced before my eyes, and I thought how utterly damn silly it would be for me to get killed while trying to cut down this sail. I tossed and turned and hated the thought of going over the top at dawn. But it was not long before I could make out the shape of the bunk

Length overall	43′ (13·1 m.)	Length waterline	36′	(11·00 m.)
Beam	17′ (5·19 m.)	Draft	1·83′	(0·558 m.)
Displacement	3·5 tons	Sail area	950 sq. ft.	(88·5 sq. m.)

Skipper: Bill Howell. *Designer*: Rudy Choy. *Builder*: Contour Craft, Great Yarmouth.

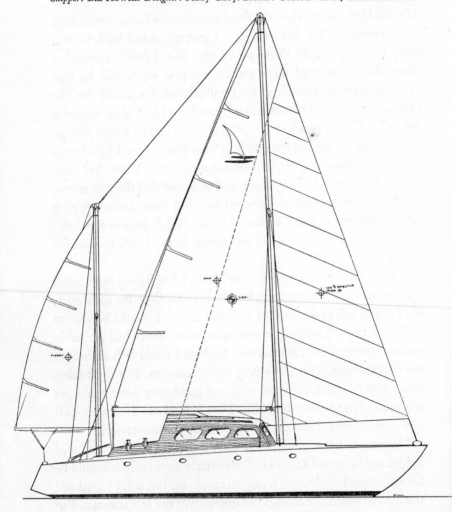

15A. *Golden Cockerel*: Sail plan.

128

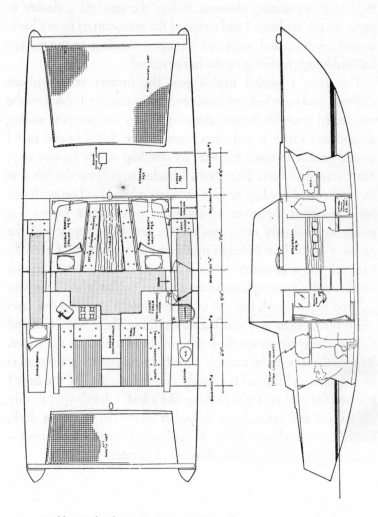

15B. *Golden Cockerel:* Arrangement and Profile

Golden Cockerel is very different from the *Pen Duick IV* and *Cheers* because she has quite spacious accommodation. Typical of Rudy Choy's catamarans, she has a comparatively narrow beam.

opposite and I went on deck to watch the first shafts of eastern light with an uneasy pleasure. Before the sun had a chance to show up my tardiness I had strapped the wire-cutters to my back, bound my hand and wrist and was again standing on the mizzen halliard winch reaching up the luff of the sail.

This time I hauled myself past the jumper tang without difficulty and soon had my hands over the spreaders. I rested on the windward spreader before shinning up to the jumper, sliding around and on to it and then resting there. I had hoped that I would be able to reach the wire by standing on the jumper stay, but I was just over a foot short. I hauled myself up the last few feet and curled my legs around the mast while I held on with one hand and used the other to undo the wire-cutters. *Lipton* was going more slowly now, but the sea was still choppy and the pitching of the boat brought my heart into my mouth. Carefully I moved the wire-cutters around in front of me and tucked one handle under an armpit and struck home on the other. The wire halliard was bruised, but not cut. Laboriously I opened the jaws of the blades again and struck a second time. There was a rush and the sail was lying on the deck with the head trailing in the water. 'Now's the time to be careful.' Slowly I strapped the wire-cutters to my back and slipped cautiously down the mast. By the time I reached the cockpit I was shaking like a leaf. I didn't wait to tidy up the sail and instead just slipped it under the straps on deck, tacked *Lipton* and went below to my bunk. I slept for four hours— twice as long as any nap since leaving Plymouth.

23. Position: 600 miles west of Land's End,

24. Alain Gliksman's iceberg. Four competitors saw a total of eight icebergs. The icing during the winter of 1967–68 was particularly severe and this increased the number of icebergs in the race area during June. Noel Bevan in *Myth of Malham* came closest to collision when he was forced downwind towards an iceberg in a gale. To get to Newport by the shortest route it is necessary to cross the iceberg zone and it seems only a matter of time before a yacht hits one.

12

Three Days of Deep Depression

The Gods spared me early on Friday morning, but they were in a sullen mood and the news from London was not good and the sailing to follow was even worse. I was immeasurably depressed. Alex Faulkner—*The Daily Telegraph* correspondent in New York —had telephoned David Thorpe to say that I was probably lying fourth. The news knocked me into silence. Apparently *Myth of Malham* was leading, followed by *Voortrekker*, *Cheers* and *Raph*. I slumped back in my seat and tried to fathom why such a small boat should be doing so well. I knew that *Myth* had often beaten boats much larger than herself in races with the R.O.R.C. and it had taken me a long time to overhaul her just west of the Lizard on the second day out. For a few hours my faith in the large boat for singlehanded sailing was shaken and I was forced to understand that a smaller boat kept at her maximum speed could beat a bigger vessel. But I had kept *Lipton* to his maximum speed! I could see no sense in any boat being ahead of me. I was not to know that these sightings were based on surmise, that the U.S. Navy aircraft which saw me yesterday had failed to identify my number and that the friends of the other yachts all claimed that their horse was in front!

Saturday, June 22nd

The north-wester did not materialise, and I was plagued with winds that made me tack east of due south in order to clear the coast. Saturday night brought headwinds of forty knots and found me slaving on deck, soaked to the skin and working without a will. I no longer went about my jobs with a light heart.

The news about Hurricane Brenda was far from encouraging. Apparently it was curving round to the north and could reach my area by Tuesday. I felt that I was much too close to the Nova Scotia shore and decided to tack south to give myself more sea room. The pilots say that the Labrador current can set towards the north-east after prolonged south-west winds and it was just my luck to find the current setting against me now.

Sunday, June 23rd

On Sunday I missed my call to London by being kept busy on deck, but later I sent a radio-telegram. I could imagine David Thorpe having to tell Father that I had not telephoned and leaving him to spend a very uneasy Sunday with no work to distract him. I imagined that most of the other competitors would be well south of me, and I envied them their unrestricted sailing as I fought between two shores and against an unfavourable current. Although my daily runs through the water were almost up to the average for the voyage, my distance made good to Newport was dismally poor. I seemed to be trimming *Lipton's* sails and self-steering gear badly and I could not point him high into the wind. *Thomas* sensed my mood and was being awkward in sympathy. The thought that I might be slipping from fourth to fifth place was almost too much to bear. In my depressed state of mind I seemed to be very prone to accidents. Until now I had not hurt myself, but the depression of losing encouraged me to burn myself on the primus, to come close to knocking myself out on the mainboom, to repeatedly fall on deck, to tear my oilskins in three places and my hands in two. There was no doubt in my mind that being depressed and accident-prone were inexplicably linked.

T. E. Lawrence was also in a poor position. It had started well enough in the excitement of the Hejaz campaign during those tense days at the beginning of the race when everything was so new. The hard work of the first week was rewarded by being first to Akaba and the voyage continued to follow the ups and downs of Lawrence's life in the desert. Now we were in a flat period waiting for the final push to Damascus.

In the long watches of Sunday night, while a gale blew itself up and out, I mused about the consequences of finishing fourth. Clearly I had failed, but would that not be better for someone of tender years? If I won there would be a certain amount of publicity. Might this not spoil me into thinking that I was something I was not? And, having achieved what I wanted, would I not want to sit back and relax?

During the race my mind had been moving steadily towards working in some sail training organisation on return to England. Would this be easier or more difficult if I lost the race? There was little doubt that it would be more difficult, but losing might have unseen compensations.

13

Damascus

Monday, June 24th

Radio telegram to *Sir Thomas Lipton* via Radio Halifax:

At 1805 hours Canadian aircraft reported June 23rd. Myth 44 m. SE of St. John. Raph retired. 1747 hours Voortrekker 43 05N 59 28W. Sir Thomas Lipton 43 40N 61 15W. Congratulations. Go it! Thorpe.

I bounced across the cabin shrieking like a schoolboy and was quickly brought to my senses when I banged my head on a deck beam. I transferred these positions to the chart to find that *Lipton* was sixty miles ahead of *Voortrekker*. I made one hundred excuses why *Voortrekker* could get to Newport ahead of me but reason dictated that if I was still sixty miles ahead after the four bad days, I would have been a hundred miles ahead on Thursday, which meant that I had a boat which was basically faster, and, barring accidents, I should reach Newport first. But to apply reason to matters not directly concerned with the running of the boat I have always found difficult in the refined atmosphere of a ship at sea. I was now less than three hundred miles from Newport and passing eighty miles south of Cape Sable.

On Monday night I had one and a half hours' sleep and spent the rest of the time monitoring the boat's progress. Just after dawn I took a short nap, and when I woke up some premonition carried me into the cockpit before checking the log and compass. As I climbed through the hatch I was presented with a scene that made my heart miss a beat. Less than two cables' length astern was a gaggle of eight Russian trawlers and I could see no clear path between them. The line of my wake seemed to point at the side of the nearest trawler and I thanked my lucky stars that the Colonel's innocence had chosen a clear path. Somehow, *Lipton* had wormed clear of these boats and I expect it was their sirens which had woken me up. For the first time in the race tiredness was beginning to take its toll and for three nights now I had gone to sleep with the generator running and the lights on to stop me sleeping too long. The off-course alarm and my alarm clock were failing to rouse me.

Tuesday, June 25th

Tuesday suited my mood. The sky was clear and *Lipton* was reaching through a blue sea at nine knots. A school of forty porpoises swam alongside the boat and played tag with the vessel's cut water. The danger of Hurricane Brenda was past and I had heard WQXR—one of New York's Radio Stations—announce that *Thomas Lipton* was leading in the Transatlantic Solo Race. Obviously knighthoods were not recognised in the States. I wondered if the friends I had known in New York knew that I was competing in the race.

At tea-time I spent a few minutes explaining the situation to *Sir Thomas*. After some close questioning he said that he understood my urgency to get to Newport and promised to work as hard as he knew how. I fully expected him to slack and kept a close eye on his movements, but for the next few hours I could see that he was giving his best so I egged him on with kind words about marinas and warm waters and admiring spectators and pretty visitors and washes and neatly stowed kit . . . I had no need to go on. *Thomas* understood, surfed off the first wave that

VOORTREKKER

Length overall	49·25′ (15 m.)	Length waterline	39·5′ (12 m.)
Beam	11·50′ (3·5 m.)	Draft	8·16′ (2·5 m.)
Displacement	6·5 tons	Sail area	900 sq. ft. (82·2 sq. m.)
Percentage ballast	52%		

Skipper: Bruce Dalling. *Designer*: E. G. van de Stadt. *Builders*: Thesens, Knysna, Cape Province.

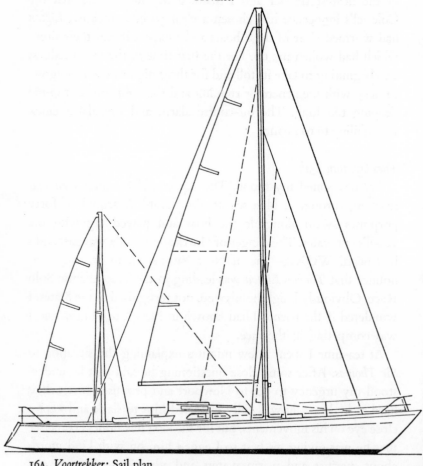

16A. *Voortrekker:* Sail plan

Voortrekker This is probably the lightest off-shore racer of 50 ft. length hull and the weight is concentrated amidships and in a very low-slung keel. equipped with a release catch in case one of them should prove impossible to very shallow and this must have made her a lively boat to sail. Bruce Dalling due to the boat's quick motion.

16B. *Voortrekker:* Arrangement and Profile

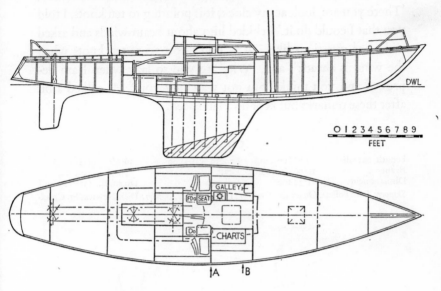

16C. *Voortrekker:* Sections

SECTION A

SECTION B

overall which has ever been built. She is well constructed with a cold-moulded
Dalling carried five spinnakers for running and the spinnaker halliard was
hand. The extremely light displacement means that the sections have to be
was extremely tired on arrival at Newport and this might have been partly

came his way and smiled through a glowing bow wave as if to say, 'There you are, look at my clock, it is pointing to ten knots, I told you that I could do it.' I chided him about beam winds and asked awkward questions like, 'Why don't you go at ten knots when the wind is ahead?', and, 'Why are you so lazy when I am depressed and you think I am not watching you?' He sulked a bit after these remarks but kept up a fair speed.

CHEERS

Length overall	40·0′ (12·2 m.)	Length waterline	36·0′	(11·0 m.)
Beam	16·66′ (5·07 m.)	Draft	4·25′	(1·3 m.)
Displacement	1·34 tons	Sail area	340 sq. ft.	(31·6 sq. m.)

Skipper: Tom Follett. *Owner and Designer*: Dick Newick. *Builder*: Dick Newick, St. Croix·

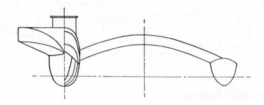

17. *Cheers*: Section.
On trials in the Caribbean, *Cheers* capsized and Tom Follett found it impossible to right her when she was floating upside down. He was rescued by a tramp steamer and on returning to St. Croix added the bubble to prevent a capsize in the race. *Cheers* was exceptionally well built with hulls of cold-moulded $\frac{3}{4}''$ mahogany and laminated spruce cross members. Both in accommodation and rig she was kept light and simple and her deck equipment comprised only two small winches and a few cleats. The area between the hulls was spanned by nylon webb netting instead of a bridged deck.

After sunset he tried to surprise me by setting the sea on fire. I was back on the counter adjusting the self-steering so that there would be less strain on his tiller when I chanced to look down and there was a stark white line every bit as sensational as lightning. The keel was leaving a trail of phosphorescence and I was pleased

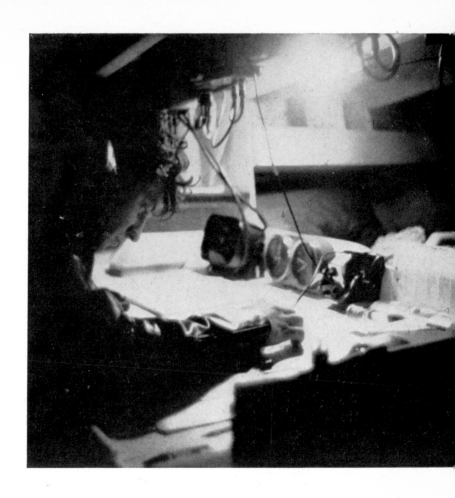

25. At the chart table. My overriding concern was *Lipton*'s position in the race. I was continually analysing the weather and trying to work out how these conditions would be affecting the other boats.

27. There was no thought of vanquishing one's opponents because winning depended on so much luck, and had that subtle lady waved her wand in another direction then all those occasions when I might have driven the boat a little faster, a little farther, would come flooding before my eyes to torture my dreams and stick pins in my memory.

26. Half way through the afternoon I heard the heavy drone of an aircraft and went up to see a Shackleton of Coastal Command circling the boat. After three circuits he flew off to the south and I watched to see if he started to circle again and show me the position of another boat. He disappeared over the horizon and I went back to my sickbed.

28. As soon as I passed the finishing line *Lipton* would be obsolete and my fascination with him would come to an end.

29. For a while, losing the sails seemed to make no difference; but slowly the log started to fall and after an age *Lipton* was still; still for the first time in three and a half weeks. It was all over.

30. Coming alongside at Newport.

31. For the first few hours ashore I was full of subconscious memories of the race—I walke
in a high bouncing style as if I was continually trying to step over a boom and my
conversation was full of radio telephone jargon such as 'over' and 'do you read me?'

32. I suppose we had both taken a pride in the way we sprang around our boats during the race and now, in the warm sunshine, with no heavy clothes to clog our movements, it was so satisfying to watch my own ballet reflected in Bruce Dalling's movements as he swept across the deck to attend to some detail before it had caught my eye.

to see that *Sir Thomas's* parent had had the wit to make this a clear-cut line rather than a messy plume which would have pointed to an unfair shape.

Just before dinner I had another nap and came on deck to find the weather muggy and close and the wind playing truant again. I cursed the naughty boy. Of all days to run away—just when I needed him most! I whistled and tampered with the sails and the self-steering. All to no avail. I had visions of being trapped in the pit of a deep low with Bruce Dalling tearing along in the northern sector at ten knots. Oh my God, ten hours of this behaviour and Bruce would be ahead of me. Please, wind, please come back again! The wind made rude gestures, remained obdurate and sent his best friend—lightning—to cheer me up. Great trees of fork lightning plunged into the sea with almighty explosions while *Sir Thomas* was left neglected and still.

After an hour, these appalling pyrotechnics had me rummaging in the textbooks trying to work out if my metal mast was a saviour or a liability. I was still unsure when the lightning ran off and left me with a dense fog. This was the sort of stuff they use for effect in Sherlock Holmes films. I could almost cut the murk with a knife. Once more my mainmast retreated from my vision and still the blasted wind frolicked in other places. It was totally silent—a heavy thick silence to match the fog. I went below to eat noodles and steamed pudding and, somehow, they mirrored the night.

As I am finishing my coffee there is a faint sound of rumbling. It is just like the last Tube thundering beneath the street only two blocks away. But this Tube train is headed in my direction! What is more, it is not safely underground but afloat, and made of steel and weighing ten thousand tons and very nasty to meet on such a night. The heavy roar of diesel motors thuds through the gloom and I watch my grey smoky walls with considerable apprehension. At last the sound starts to die away. 'Thank God, that was a big one,' I say to myself as I wait and watch for the swell. But the swell does not come and now the diesels are thudding their way back again. At any minute I expect to see a knife of steel some thirty feet high and travelling at eighteen knots pierce through the gloom and my hull in quick succession. Life-raft. Grabbed and put in cockpit. The noise goes away again but after a few minutes it starts to work itself up into a grand crescendo. The last time that every pore of my body acted like an exposed electrode was outside Damascus during the rioting in July 1963. Some Syrian soldiers at a remote Army post had stopped our Land-Rover, roughly questioned us and had laid us on canvas camp beds with our hands behind our heads. We were wearing shorts and desert boots and did not like being searched by these soldiers who seemed to be fascinated by our Oxford white skin. But this brown hand which had come to seek me out will not even know if he cuts me in two! The diesels start to recede, the wash rolls in, I am safe again . . . as I was in Syria. But I was not to know that when it all started!

Wednesday, June 26th

Midnight brings another day and some welcome wind, but no sleep. For all the hours of darkness I sit at my chart table and plan my tactics for crossing the shoals. Because I went so far north when my mizzen staysail jammed aloft and because *Voortrekker's* last position was south of my track I imagine that all the competitors are to the south of me. I chew this over and plan my course so that whatever the wind does my track tends to keep them outside me on the longer arc to Newport. I listen to all the weather forecasts, check the tide tables. It has been blowing from the south and south-west on and off for three days so I must expect a strong tidal surge out of the Bay of Fundy. That means that I can head to the north and expect the current to carry me south of my heading. David Thorpe and I rejoice that this might well be the last radio contact, because at six o'clock I am 180 miles from Newport.

After daybreak the wind gets up to twenty-five knots from the south. It is far enough round to set the staysail. *Lipton* is enjoying himself at over ten knots and I fear for the safety of my big jib. If I were any more than a day from the finish, I would change down.

Just before midday the wind swings back so quickly that the self-steering is only beginning to pull the boat around when the mainsail starts to swing across. The end of the boom is already ravishing the bloom of the staysail as I take an extra turn on the foreguy. Somehow I manage to get the boat to head off to the south, down the staysail, gybe and up the staysail again. Now the wind is beginning to roar at well over thirty knots from the starboard quarter.

I dash below to work out how long this wind will have to hold to see me across the Nantucket Shoals. If this wind keeps up for five hours then I will have the benefit of the ebbtide and the wind pushing off the shallow water. I draw a red line around the four-fathom mark and take a bearing on the most northerly four-fathom passage through the shoals. This takes me fourteen miles north of the Light and right past the Davis Shoal can buoy. If the wind dies away or changes direction then I will be forced to sail off to the south to avoid running aground. Back on deck the band is in full swing. I spend an hour tending sheets and trimming the boat for its best performance before returning to the chart table to plot my course. Already the sea is steep and angry, and at times *Lipton* was suspended between the crests of the waves. Water boils up above the counter and screeches off the sheer of the bows. The speedometer is held at eleven and a quarter knots for over ten minutes. At the chart table I take a series of Loran positions which all cross in a point. Half an hour later I take another set which again cross in a point and agree with the dead reckoning and depth sounder. The underwater banks are beginning to show up and their position agrees exactly with the dead reckoning. For three hours I work like a demon splitting my time equally between the chart table and the cockpit. I have to use my arms and mind in equal proportions. This is sailing at its best.

I start to call Castle Hill coastguard station at Newport to report my position. There is a good deal of traffic and I only get through at the third attempt. Bill Muesel takes my messages and promises to pass them on to Alex Faulkner who is waiting for me in Newport. At the end of the conversation Bill asks me to hold. I wait for three minutes and he comes through again loud and clear. 'The race official, Lieutenant-Colonel Odling-Smee, says that you should pass south of the Nantucket Light Vessel, but you appear to be going north of it.' I reply that my sailing instructions say pass south of Nantucket, but I will check these again and call back in five minutes. Even if I do have to go south of the Light it will all be downwind work and should not add more than an hour and a half to my time, but I am sure that the instructions say 'south of Nantucket'. I pull them out on the chart table and check them again. Once more I check the Pilot book and after five minutes call Castle Hill. 'My sailing instructions definitely say—pass south of Nantucket, not Nantucket Light Vessel, repeat the written instructions say pass south of Nantucket—full stop. What shall I do?' Bill asks me to hold while he checks with Odling-Smee. 'Odling-Smee says that you must do what your written sailing instructions say'. 'Very good, I will pass north of the Light and just south of the four-fathom mark on the shoals. E.T.A. 1000 hours G.M.T. tomorrow.' Bill mutters something about the shoals being dangerous and signs off. 'Is there anyone else in yet?'

I ask, as casually as I know how. Bill waits some time, confers with Odling-Smee and replies laconically, 'No, no one else yet.' Relief.

I am sure that if I had lived in this part of the world and heard the tales about 'the dangerous Nantucket Shoals' then I would not have dreamt of driving *Lipton* so high across them. But lacking this experience and basing my judgment on what I could find on the chart and in the pilot books I thought it was a justifiable risk.

By this time the gale had reached its maximum and regretfully I hauled down the mizzen staysail or else I would have been left with only a luff wire. It was such a beautiful sail that I could not bear to see it torn. The wind veered a couple of points and *Lipton* was now running before it. In incredibly confused seas the boat ran as straight as a die with practically no rolling and with the big jib winging itself out to windward without the help of the boom. And we had been worried about *Thomas*'s directional stability! The anemometer recorded forty knots for more than an hour and the gusts soared to over the fifty mark. Now that the wind was more directly astern the boat's speed dropped to ten knots. The sight of the sea waves was so appalling as they piled themselves on to the submarine banks that I didn't dare to look at them for longer than a few minutes and thanked God that I had lids to cover my eyes. By using the Loran, the depth sounder, the log and the compass together I reckoned that I could fix my position to within half a cable. To north and south there were acres of white foaming seas where the shallower banks were causing the waves to break furiously. *Lipton* rode past with the bearing of a king.

Just before dark I slipped below to work out my latest position. I suppose I was out of the cokpit for ten minutes and when I came back on deck I was startled to see a small American fishing boat with its nets set less than fifty yards to starboard. I could easily see the incredulous expression on the two fishermen's faces as they blankly looked at me then at one another, then stared at me some more. In no time I was gone in a plume of spray which must have obscured the hull to leave a fatherless rig dancing above the surf.

I was getting very excited and had to revert to my bare survival rations. Tummy would not stand for more. Radio-telegram to Alex Faulkner:

Position at 2030 G.M.T. 40 45N 69 38W. Course 280 degrees true at 9 knots. Ninety miles to go—stop—Can you meet me with towing launch—stop—will advise coastguard of E.T.A. closer to finish—could be Thursday 0800 G.M.T.

I don't remember eating a meal that evening. By 2200 G.M.T. I was clear of the Davis Shoal and shaping a course for a point eight miles south of Nomans Island. The next four hours passed in a happy haze and at 0220 hours G.M.T. I called the coastguard station at Castle Hill.

Thursday, June 27th

I gave them a revised E.T.A. of 0600 hours which would mean that I would arrive in the middle of their night. Halfway through the conversation I asked if there were any other boats which had arrived in Newport. This time my voice betrayed a note of urgency. 'No, Captain, no other boats yet.' By way of compensation for calling my boat 'Thomas Lipton', I was always given the prefix 'Captain'. Vaguely, I remembered the training needed to become a captain in either the Navy or Merchant Service in England and blushed at my new title.

Two hours went by without incident and I soaked up the feeling of being alone with *Lipton* at sea. It would never be like this again.

I had still seen no landmarks since leaving the Scillies and my tired imagination started to play ducks and drakes with my navigation. Just suppose that there was some progressive error built into my navigation over the last three thousand seven hundred miles! Just suppose that the depth soundings and Loran lines of positions coincided with other sandbanks and other transmitting stations miles away from where I imagined myself to be. Just imagine that all my celestial sights had been wrong and the log had an error of twenty per cent, then I might be rushing on to the shore with a following gale in the St. Lawrence River, Chespeake Bay, the entrance to New York Harbour, or just anywhere! It was a frightening nightmare but not altogether preposterous considering that I had relied on artificial aids for three and a half weeks and not once had I seen a landmark and said with conviction, 'Ah, we must be ten miles south-west of so and so.'

With these fantasies buzzing around my mind I waited for the sweep of Buzzard's Light. If all my thousands of calculations, graphs, plottings and surmises over the past twenty-five days were correct, it should show up fifty-five degrees off the starboard bow at 0450. It was 0440. To pass the time before this moment of reckoning, I went forward and pulled out my fenders and mooring warps. Neurosis drove me to the glucose tin. As I waited out the last few minutes I realised that to produce the fenders was a very confident move. There they were on the cabin sole dutifully waiting to nudge the edge of some secure marina. While these dumb things stared at me, I felt sure that the land would never show up. It was rather like watching a kettle that was too self-conscious to come to the boil. In the end their dull complacence, their unquestioning confidence in my confidence, got the better of me, and I kicked them out of sight and went up on deck to have a look round. That did the trick. At 0457 I picked up the flash of Buzzard's Light. I got out the hand-held compass and measured the bearing: fifty degrees.

Down below again I warmed up the transmitter and called Castle Hill. I opened with 'Are there any other boats in yet?' 'No, Captain, you are the first, no other boats in yet.' I told them that I had picked up the Buzzard's Light. I told them that this was the first mark I had seen, that I should be at the Brenton Tower in less than three hours, that my navigation lights were smashed and that I would leave the receiver tuned in for messages from them.

The wind had lightened and now that I was in a land-locked stretch of water the direction of the wind kept varying and I was busy adjusting the self-steering. Eventually the wind settled down from a direction ahead of the beam and I had to drop the mizzen to stop over-powering the boat. Because I was using the topping lift as a mizzen halliard the boom limped sadly to the deck.

At 0610 the mass of flashing and multicoloured lights in and around Newport rose to view above the horizon. How ironic, I thought, that this race should end in Newport, that summer summit of the East Coast where to go yachting is a flamboyant symbol to colour your blood a darker shade of blue. Of all places in North America, this one represents a way of life so different from our own. Here everything militates against the whims of the individual, to do something different is to 'drop out' and to lead a spartan existence is queer. This race might not appeal to the Americans. I was still too far away to pick out the Brenton Reef and this promised to be a difficulty against the psychedelic background.

Castle Hill confirmed that no boats had been seen, and now I could look across a bare stretch of black water to the finishing line at the Brenton Tower. At last I knew I was going to win! Not then, nor after the finish, did I think about the twelve-hour penalty. I knew, and the other competitors knew, that I had left Plymouth with no unfair advantage over them. We were out there, we knew in our souls the order of things. It was part of us and no machinations could ever alter what we felt. The race was an intensely personal thing with oneself, not a contest with other people—they were only there as an indicator of how the will of Geoffrey Williams had fared in its contest with the slothful body of Geoffrey Williams. To take an advantage over one's opponents in a race of this kind was to violate one's own being. It was quite unthinkable. I was going to cross the line first which meant that as things go, I had done quite well. There was no thought of vanquishing one's opponents, because the victory depended on so much luck, and had this subtle lady waved her wand in another direction then all those occasions when I might have driven the boat a little harder, a little farther, would come flooding before my eyes to torture my dreams and to stick pins in my memory. But everyone who finished had won and everyone had lost because it was impossible to live as one wanted for twenty-five days, thirty days, thirty-five days or even one day.

I had been lucky, and by winning there would be no need for me to hold courts-martial in the secret chambers of my mind. But if the truth be known I am sure that other competitors had given as much and much more than I myself. Because the world would not understand this more subtle, more important race, then too many people would be frustrated and disappointed. Cups, trophies, speeches and dinners—I wanted none of this and I prayed that the second man home would give himself the grace of twelve hours to spare him at a time when he would be so vulnerable.

A ferry crossed my course and I had to pay off to avoid him. By 0700, or 2 a.m. local time, I could see a flotilla of boats heading my way with the Brenton Reef Light still very faint behind them. *Lipton* seemed to want to fall off below the light and I went aft to stand by the vane. The closer I got to the light the more I had to head into the wind and the direction was varying so much that I stayed on the counter to keep resetting the vane. It would not have been typical of the voyage for me to steer the boat across the finishing line. The nearest boat was less than a hundred yards away, but still the crew had not seen me. Then there was a shout and the high-powered searchlights swept the deck and the sails. When it shone on 'No. 44' I could hear some people say 'It's *Lipton*!' Now, motor-boats swept in for a closer look and I was told the coastguard cutter would tow me into the harbour. I was surprised that so many boats had come out this late.

Only a quarter of a mile now and the flotilla had turned round to accompany me. I well remember making a conscious effort to savour those last few minutes because they marked the end of my affair with *Lipton*. This boat was built for one person, at one time and for one race, and although I knew less about singlehanded sailing now than when I started, one thing was certain: as soon as I passed the finishing line *Lipton* would be obsolete and my fascination with this beautiful thing would come to an end. It is a sad thing to hear people say that they love a boat. Is this all she can do? Just demand an unquestioning love? One should feel elation, depression, fear. . . . How dull just to love a boat.

Tearfully, I passed the Tower at 7.30 G.M.T. We rode on together for a few minutes and then I went forward and dropped all the sails into untidy heaps on the deck. For a while, losing the sails seemed to make no difference; but slowly the log started to fall, and after an age *Lipton* was still. Still for the first time in three and a half weeks. Now it was all over and I was completely satisfied.

14

Epilogue

A crewman on the coastguard cutter threw me a heaving line and within seconds a warp was snaking through the black water. It took the strain on Lipton's bows and I went below to switch off the yacht's instruments. I wanted to pat Thomas on his neck and tell him what a good horse he had been, but I couldn't decide which part of him was the neck so I stood idly in the companionway wondering what to do.

The chronometer caught my eye and reminded me that it was time for my daily call to *The Daily Telegraph*. 'Yes, let's wake up Thorpe,' I muttered and fell to fiddling with the coloured knobs. While the set whirred and warmed itself I watched the lights of the bay twinkling through the main hatch. Suddenly the lights went out and only slowly did I recognise the profile of a motor-boat outlined in black against an even blacker sky. This launch did not seem to be part of the flotilla of spectator boats which were now streaming ahead of the coastguard cutter. It looked as if it had followed me in from the open sea. Now I could see two people standing and peering.

'Geoffrey !'

There was no mistaking the owner of the voice. It belonged to Paul Dana who had been my pupil at St. Bernard's and who had cruised with me in the Virgin Islands. I scampered back on to the counter to find that the boat's driver was Mike Westgate who had been mate on the second West Indies expedition. Mike swept the launch in close on my port quarter and I grabbed Paul as he strode across the moving gap between the vessels. He was the first person to puncture the privacy of my cabin and I could think of no one better. As we reached the brighter water of the harbour Paul slipped back on board the launch to avoid speculation about my having a crew and embarrassment with the Customs.

The cutter shunted *Lipton* into the marina at 4.30 a.m. local time. There were about a hundred people on the dock and I was delighted to see Gardy Barker waiting on the pontoon. I was even more pleased to see how thrilled he was at the recent turn of events. Gardy and the Customs officer came on board and we settled the formalities in record time. I stepped ashore with my suitcase and the idea of quietly retiring to an hotel. But I was not to get away with it that easily! I was collared by a group of reporters and their questions kept me jabbering for hours and hours. This was no hardship because after twenty-five days of talking to myself I was quite keen to practise on other people.

The cables, 'phone calls and friends kept arriving at the dock all day and I was interrogated, shaken by the hand, hugged, kissed and photographed in furious succession. Even the siren of Newport beach turned up to see how *Thomas* had flaunted the dreams that she had inspired. The guitar player from the marina bar took one look at *Lipton*'s low freeboard, immediately rearranged the words of the Beatles' song and serenaded the dock with 'We all live in a blue and white submarine'.

Alex Faulkner had come up from New York, and late that afternoon we all retired to the Castle Hill Hotel which overlooks the entrance to Newport Harbour.

I was in a deep sleep when some part of my brain which I had forgotten to switch off with the Harrier log and the other instruments suddenly startled me with the sound of a bell ringing on a buoy. I bounded out of bed and rushed to the window. Oh, my

God, so near to the finish but so far from finishing. My befuddled eyes focused on steep rocks and waves, scattered beaches and green lawns. I cursed my bad luck in running aground, so close to the finish. Slowly, I remembered that I *had* won, that it *is* all over and that I am supposed to be resting instead of trying to sail my bed around the bedroom. I went back to bed but couldn't sleep, and as soon as it was light I took my second, luxurious shower, wrote an article for the *Telegraph* and wandered out on to the lawns. It was so good to smell the flowers, and the grass again, to run through the bushes until I was puffed, to swim in the sea knowing that I could leave it at any moment I liked. On my way back from the beach, I paused for breath under some low trees and looked out into the channel to see a coastguard cutter come out of the foliage towing a yellow, banana shaped toy. Tom Follett was hunched on one float, with his yellow sailing jacket covering his short neck. He looked dejected and forlorn. No sirens for him, no peering motor-launches, no eager pressmen, no one to meet him. He passed within a hundred yards and I wanted to rush over to him to explain how unfair it all was. He had won as well, it didn't matter if the other people didn't understand. But then I realised that no matter what I said he wouldn't be too pleased to see me. Not yet, anyway. With this thought, I hid myself in the bushes to be sure that he did not catch sight of me. When he had gone, I ran back to the hotel for breakfast.

For some days I thought that Tom was second, but Bruce Dalling had come in the previous evening. There can be no doubt that Tom's crossing in *Cheers* was the most phenomenal performance in the race, but they didn't win and I was sad to think about what he and the other competitors felt. But the sadness didn't seem to last long. Soon, I heard of their plans for the next trans-atlantic race, the Round Britain Race, for sailing around the world alone. Once some new carrot started to swing redly in the haze of their imagination, then their interest seeped back again. People always seem happier in the past or the future. The present rarely appears exciting.

Although all my instincts wanted to carry me away from *Lipton* I did have one more sail on him before returning to England. Paul Dana, Bruce Dalling and some friends from New York came as crew, and it was a pleasant relief to have other people help work the boat.

After so long at sea one becomes supremely well co-ordinated with the boat's gear and movements. I suppose Bruce and I had both taken a pride in the way we sprang around our boats during the race and now, in the warm sunshine, with no heavy clothes to clog our movements, it was so satisfying to see my own ballet reflected in Bruce's movements as he swept across the deck like a nimble-footed cat. As we slipped back into our narrow berth at the marina, Bruce and I worked the boat with a deftness and speed which surprised ourselves as much as the onlookers. *Lipton* behaved himself and settled against the dock without a murmur.

During the months of preparation Robert and I decided that my attitude during the race would be more like that of a sprinter than a marathon runner if I did not have to sail the boat back to England. Happily, the Royal Military Academy, Sandhurst, agreed to sail the boat home so I flew back to England three weeks after arriving in Newport.

The post-race celebrations came to a climax when I returned to Cornwall. To my amazement the Camborne-Redruth Urban District Council laid on a reception in a dance hall near my home. Although Redruth is geographically close to the sea, in terms of interest in sailing it is as far removed as Birmingham or Huddersfield and I was touched by the warmth of local people's feelings.

By now it was late July and from then until early October my spirits fell like some stricken bird. Occasionally my morale soared to its former height and one of these flights was set off by Captain Neil Carlier bringing *Lipton* back into Falmouth after crossing from Nantucket to Land's End in eighteen days. All the crew members were as happy as crickets and full of stories about *Lipton* surfing at fifteen knots and amazement that no one had been sick for the entire crossing. After a return trip across the Atlantic the vessel looked no worse for wear than if it had been out for a trip around the bay. The crew soon cleaned and tidied the boat before returning to their homes, and they left me even more depressed than before.

At the finish I was fitter and harder than I had ever been, but now I was tired, lethargic, full of colds, asthma and swollen glands. I spent long hours in bed trying to replace the energy that I thought I had lost, but this made me even more tired than before. But it was no physical illness that was afflicting me. The trouble was that I had won the race, and now that I had reached this pinnacle which had seemed so inaccessible for so long I didn't know what to make of it.

With slow shock I came to realize that sailing could never be the same again. The details of those twenty-five days at sea were quite forgotten as they ran together into a euphoric haze of total contentment. This warm, furry thing called memory that I held so dearly was too precious to be challenged by another race. Even if I was lucky enough to win again, the sweet smell of '68 could never be repeated because there is only one first time. My reasons for entering this race had been so singular that to compete again would be positively immoral. I had tasted the elixir of working one's mind and body together in total concentration and in total application. I had felt all my senses heightened by that time at sea and now I lamented its passing and missed not being able to look forward to my great adventure. I knew that more serious things were planned to take its place, but I did not know what these were to be.

During the early autumn I drove around England visiting a number of schools, Outward Bound projects and sail training establishments. The Ocean Youth Club appealed to me most because it seemed to match the mood of young people in 1968. Also it seemed to understand that it is impossible to train character and the best one can do is to provide an environment which can change a young person's attitude to life. For eight years the club has been operating from Brightlingsea, Gosport and Plymouth. It takes young boys and girls to sea in medium-size cruising vessels for periods of between two days and two months. The club is financed and run by the young people with the minimum amount of supervision from adults needed to ensure their safety. The club's boats are old, expensive to maintain and not designed for club work. Happily I have been taken on by the club to replace the fleet with new glass-fibre ketches. So it is back to Robert again, back to sponsorship, back to the hopes and dis-appointments. It will be the *Lipton* story all over again and this time success is even more important because so many people will be involved.

If I lived by the coast I would waste my time watching the silly waves come flopping on to the beach. So I have settled on Cranborne Chase in Dorset where my only link with the sea is the gulls which come winging up to Furzey Down when a gale is blowing in the Channel. But no longer can they make me pace around the room wondering what it would be like out there in *Lipton*.

No longer can I feel a catch in my throat when I remember winter storms beating against the North Cliffs in Cornwall.

Now I can go secretly at dusk and watch the deer, the badger and the hare, returning to my dark and lonely home and no longer notice that I am alone.

It seems that I have reached the island in the granite pool of my boyhood.

Acknowledgements

Without the financial backing of Liptons this venture would not have been possible. I am deeply grateful to Malcolm Cooper of Allied Suppliers Ltd, Richard Page of Lipton (Retail) Ltd, Alec Riches of Lipton (Overseas) Ltd and Gardy Barker of Lipton Inc in the U.S.A.

Derek Kelsall developed the sandwich method of construction in this country and he must take the credit for building *Sir Thomas Lipton*.

Hundreds of people and organisations were involved in this project and to all of them I would like to say 'Thank you'. Particularly to:

All the workers at the Little Stonar Boatyard and in particular Peter Bliss, Derek Champ and Jim Gilchrist.

The Daily Telegraph who employed me as a reporter for the race.

Those firms who were so generous in giving discounts, free issues or free services:

Berger, Jenson and Nicholson–Jotun Ltd for paint
Brookes and Gatehouse Ltd for their instruments
Bruce Banks Sails
Bruntons (Musselburgh) Ltd for standing rigging
B.T.R. Industries Ltd for Plasticell
Bureau Division of English Electric Ltd, The
Channel Marine for chandlery and help with the electrical wiring
Mr Cuckson for the perspex dome and generating set
Everyone at Mylor

Helly-Hansen for oilskins and a polar suit
Henri-Lloyd for oilskins
Henry Browne and Son Ltd for the cabin compass and sextant
Henry Edie and Co for casting the keel
H. J. Silley for his help with the keel
Horlicks Ltd for their expedition foods
International Paints Ltd
Lewis, Clarke Ltd for sailcloth
Lilley and Reynolds Ltd for the main compass and chronometer
Lucas Ltd for batteries
Marlow Ropes Ltd
Mashfords
Meteorological Office, The—for advice
Montague Smith Ltd for Lewmar equipment
Radio telephone station at Baldock
Rolex Watch Company, The—for the chronometer
Sandersons for antifouling
Sharp and Co for the off-course alarm
Sparlight for masts
Stevens and Carlotti Ltd for their help with the steelwork
Thames Plywood Manufacturers Ltd
Thomas Walker Ltd for the log
Turner Brothers Asbestos Ltd for glassfibre

Captain Neil Carlier and the cadets from Royal Military Academy,
  Sandhurst, who did such a magnificent job in bringing *Lipton*
  home so quickly and in such good condition.
Thank you Brian Boots and David Thorpe for all your encouragement.

All the mistakes in the text are mine alone and I would like to
thank the following for their comments: Veronica Westall, Peter
Dismore and Hilary Osborn.

I am particularly grateful to John Perkins and Anthony Howarth for taking such magnificent photographs and to *The Daily Telegraph* for allowing me to reproduce them. Chris Smith and *The Observer* have been equally creative and generous.

Acknowledgement of illustration sources

PHOTOGRAPHS

Daily Telegraph, Anthony Howarth, plates numbers 1, 10A, 10C, 11A; *Daily Telegraph*, John Perkins, 5A, 5B, 7A, 7B, 25; *Daily Telegraph*, 27-31; *The Observer*, Chris Smith, 26, 32; *The Observer*, 14, 17A, 17B, 18, 20A, 20B, 21, 22: Photo Neptune, 12B, 15, 16, 24: Raymond Irons, 6A: Vye & Son, 6C: John Mannering, 8: Beken, 9: Eileen Ramsay, 10B: Bureau Division of English Electric Computers, 11B: *Yachting World*, 12A: Dave Evans, 13: Alain Gliksman, 23.

LINE DRAWINGS

Robert Clark (reproduced by courtesy of *Yachting World*), drawings numbers 1 and 2: *Zero Un Informative*, 6: Col. H. G. Hasler (reproduced by courtesy of Mike Richey), 7: J. Rouillard (reproduced by courtesy of *Yachting World*), 8A, 8B: H.M. Meteorological Office, 9, 11A, 11B: André Mauriac, 10A, 10B: E. G. van de Stadt (reproduced by courtesy of *Yachting World*), 12A, 12B, 16A, 16B, 16C: Hydrographic Department, Admiralty, 13: Rudy Choy, 15A, 15B: Nick Newick (reproduced by courtesy of *Yachting World*), 17.

APPENDIX I

ANALYSIS OF SAIL CHANGES AND CONDITIONS ON
SIR THOMAS LIPTON

Date – June	Boomed Staysail	Main	Mizzen	No. 2	No. 1	No. 3	Ghoster	Trysail	Mizzen Staysail	Boomed Running Sail (P)	Boomed Running Sail (S)	Beating 55° off Bow	Reaching 55°–140°	Running 140°–180°	Mean Wind Speed (k)	Mean Temperature in Cabin (°F)	Weather	Hours of Sleep	Distance Run on Log in Nautical Miles (8 a.m. to 8 a.m.)
1	X	X	X		X									X	2 / 6	59	O / S	0	90
2	X	X	X	X										X	20	55	O	4	150
	X		X	X										X	28		R		
	X	X	X	X										X	12		O		
3	X	X	X		X									X	9	54	O	4	180
	X	X	X	X										X	18		S		
	X		X	X										X	28		O		
4	X		X	X										X	18	54	O	2	143
	X	X	X	X										X	15		O		
	X	X	X		X									X	10		O		
	X	X	X	X										X	15		O		
	X	X	X					X						X	10		O		
5	X	X	X		X									X	9	53	O	4	140
	X	X	X	X										X	18		O		
	X	X	X		X									X	8		S		
6	X	X	X	X										X	14	55	S	7	185
	X		X	X										X	22		O		
7	X		X	X										X	20	58	O	4	154
	X	X	X											X	17		O		
8	X	X	X	X										X	22	59	O	5	211
9	X	X	X	X										X	15	65	S	5	166
	X	X	X	X				X					X		10		S		
	X	X	X	X										X	10		S		
	X	X	X	X				X					X		10		S		
	X	X	X	X										X	15		S		
10	X	X	X	X										X	20	51	S / O	4	180
11	X	X				X								X	25	50	O	4	142
	X		X	X										X	20		O		
12	X	X	X		X									X	15	48	O	2	134
	X	X	X	X										X	10		O		
13	X	X	X		X									X	18	50	R	4	175
	X	X	X											X	30		O		
14	X	X	X	X										X	18	48	O	4	104
	X	X	X		X								X		7		O		
15	X	X	X		X									X	2	42	F	3	43
							X		X				X		3		F		
16	X	X	X	X										X	9 / 12	42	S	6	162
	X	X	X		X									X	9		F		
17	X	X	X		X									X	9	39	S / O	4	80
	X	X	X		X					X			X		1		R / F		

Notes
Weather

O = Overcast
S = Sunny
R = Rain
F = Fog

Beaufort Scale

Less than 1k	Force 0
1 to 3k	Force 1
4 to 6k	Force 2
7 to 10k	Force 3
11 to 16k	Force 4
17 to 21k	Force 5
22 to 27k	Force 6
28 to 33k	Force 7
34 to 40k	Force 8 (Gale)
41 to 47k	Force 9
48 to 55k	Force 10 (Storm)

Date – June	Boomed Staysail	Main	Mizzen	No. 2	No. 1	No. 3	Ghoster	Trysail	Mizzen Staysail	Boomed Running Sail (P)	Boomed Running Sail (S)	Beating 55° off Bow	Reaching 55°–140°	Running 140°–180°	Mean Wind Speed (k)	Mean Temperature in Cabin (°F)	Weather	Hours of Sleep	Distance Run on Log in Nautical Miles (8a.m. to 8a.m.)
18	X	X	X	X								X			15		F		
	X	X	X		X								X		10				
	X	X	X		X				X		X			X	5				
	X	X	X		X				X	X	X			X	5				
	X	X	X		X				X	X	X			X	5	42	F	5	157
	X	X	X		X				X				X		5				
	X	X	X		X							X			7				
	X	X	X		X									X	8				
	X	X	X	X		X								X	15				
	X	X	X	X					X					X	15		F		
19	X	X	X	X								X			8		S		
	X	X	X	X								X			12				
	X	X		X								X			18	50	O	6	161
	X	X	X	X								X			15				
	X	X		X								X			20		O		
20	X	X	X	X								X			15		F		
	X	X	X		X							X			20				
	X	X	X	X								X			15		F		
	X	X		X								X			20	55		4	165
	X	X	X	X								X			17		F		
	X	X		X								X			22				
	X	X	X	X					X					X	15		F		
21	X	X	X	X								X			15		R		
	X							X				X			34	50	F	0	140
	X		X	X	X							X			18		F		
22	X	X	X	X								X			15		R		
	X	X		X								X			20	54	F	3	160
	X	X	X	X					X					X	10		S		
23	X	X	X		X							X			8	54	O	0	124
	X	X	X		X									X	8		F		
24	X	X	X		X							X			6		O		
	X	X	X		X				X					X	9	56	O	1½	137
	X	X	X		X									X	15		O		
25	X	X	X		X									X	6		F		
	X	X	X		X				X					X	6		O		
	X	X	X		X							X			5	58		1½	121
	X	X	X		X				X					X	4		O		
	X	X	X		X							X			5				
26	X	X	X		X				X					X	30		F		
	X	X	X		X									X	50	59	O	0	180
	X	X		X	X									X	30		O		
	X	X			X							X			21				

Total Distance Run =
3,784 n.m.

Great Circle Distance =
2,850 n.m.

Total number of Sail
changes – 70

APPENDIX II

RESULTS 1968 RACE

FINISHERS

		Name	Skipper	25 days	20 hours	33 min
57ft Ketch	1	Sir Thomas Lipton	Geoffrey Williams, UK	26	13	42
50ft Ketch	2	Voortrekker	Bruce Dalling, S. Africa	27	00	13
40ft Proa	3	Cheers	Tom Follett, USA	29	10	17
53ft Sloop	4	Spirit of Cutty Sark RNSA	Leslie Williams, UK	31	16	24
43ft CAT. (Ketch)	5	Golden Cockerel	Bill Howell, Aust.	34	8	23
32ft Sloop	6	Opus	Brian Cooke, UK	34	13	15
45ft TRI. (Ketch)	7	Gancia Girl	M. J. Minter-Kemp, UK	36	2	41
40ft Cutter	8	Myth of Malham RNSA	Noel Bevan, UK	37	14	47
35ft Sloop	9	Maxine	B. de Castelbajac, FR.	38	10	10
35ft Sloop	10	Maguelonne	J. Yves Terlain, FR.	38	13	13
27ft Sloop	11	Dogwatch	Nigel Burgess, UK	40	1	16
36ft Sloop	12	Silvia II (Restarted June 12*)	André Foezon, FR.	40	15	13
19ft 7in Sloop	13	Fione	B. Enbom, Sweden	41	12	46
37ft Sloop	14	Mex	Claus Hehner, W. Germ.	42	3	49
32ft Ketch	15	Rob Roy RNSA	Rev. Stephen Pakenham, UK	45	10	8
33ft TRI.	16	Startled Faun	Colin Forbes, UK	48	19	5
25ft TRI.	17	Amistad	Bernie Rodriquez, USA	57	10	48
25ft 9in Sloop	18	Jester	Michael Richey, UK	Disqualified		
19ft 7in Sloop		Goodwin II	A. Mattson, Sweden	29	16	

*Actual time

161

APPENDIX III

RESULTS 1960 AND 1964 RACES

1960
start 10.00, 11th *June*

Gipsy Moth III	F. Chichester	40d	12hr	30m
Jester	Colonel H. G. Hasler	48	12	02
Cardinal Vertue	David Lewis	55	00	50
Eira	Val Howells	62	05	50

1964
start 10.00, 23rd *May*

Pen Duick II	E. Tabarly	27d	03hr	56m
Gipsy Moth III	F. Chichester	29	23	57
Akka	Val Howells	32	18	08
Lively Lady	Alec Rose	36	17	30
Jester	Colonel H. G. Hasler	37	22	05
Stardrift	Bill Howell	38	23	23
Rehu Moana	David Lewis	38	12	04
Ilala	Mike Ellison	46	06	26
Golif	Jean Lacombe	46	07	05
Vanda Caelea	Bob Bunker	49	18	45
Misty Miller	Mike Butterfield	53	00	05
Ericht	G. Chaffey	60	11	15
Folatre	Derek Kelsall	61	14	04
Marco Polo	Axel Pedersen	63	13	30

Akka was delayed at the start, and put into S. Ireland for repairs.
Misty Miller put into the Azores for repairs.
Ericht put into the Azores for repairs.
Marco Polo left Plymouth 10.58, 26th May.
Folatre returned to Plymouth with damage and left again 12.00, 19th June.
Tammie Norrie retired.

Glossary

Anemometer—An instrument for measuring the strength of the wind.

Back, to—To sheet the clew of a sail to windward. The wind is said to back when it changes its direction contrary to the movement of the sun.

Bareheaded—To sail without a jib.

Batten—A flexible strip of wood or metal inserted in a pocket on the leech of a sail to extend the reach and prevent curling and flapping.

Beat, to—To sail to windward on a zig-zag course with the wind first on one bow and then on the other.

Block—A device for changing the lead of a rope with the minimum of friction —a landlubber's pulley.

Cable—A chain, or fibre or wire rope, by means of which a vessel rides to her anchor. Also a measure of distance, one-tenth of a nautical mile (200 yards).

Catamaran—A vessel with two hulls.

Chainplates—Metal strips on the side of a vessel to which the lower ends of a shroud or runner is secured.

Cheek—A block is made up of two plates which enclose a sheave—each plate is called a cheek.

Chine—The angle where the topside joins the bottom in a flat-bottomed or V-bottomed vessel.

Chronometer—An accurate clock used for navigation.

Consolan—A system of radio navigation which relies on interpreting a series of dots and dashes transmitted by shore beacons.

Curves—Wooden or plastic shapes used to draw curved lines.

Cutter—A fore and aft rigged vessel with one mast, a mainsail and two headsails (foresail and jib).

Displacement—The weight of a vessel.

Facsimile Receiver—An instrument which receives and displays weather maps.

Fin and Skeg profile—The profile of a yacht when the hull is a canoe body, the keel has the shape of a fin and the rudder is separated from the keel and supported by a smaller fin.

Foredeck—The deck forward of the main mast.

Foreguy—A steadying rope running from a boom forwards.

Forestay—A wire rope giving forward support to the mast.

Foretriangle—The area outlined by the forestay, the foredeck and the main mast.

Frame—A rib of a vessel.

Freeboard—The height of a vessel's side above the water.

Great Circle route—Shortest distance route between any two places on the earth's surface.

Ground gear—Gear used for anchoring.

Guardrails—Railings, usually of wire or metal pipe, supported by stanchions, to prevent a person from falling overboard.

Gunwale—The upper edge of the boat's side.

Growler—A small iceberg.

Gybe, to—When running, to bring the wind from one quarter to the other so that the boom swings across.

Halliard—A rope used for hoisting a sail or flag.

Head—The bow, also the top edge of a sail.

Jumpers—A small strut forward of the mast. A jumper stay runs over this strut and helps to keep the upper part of the mast upright.

Kedge—An anchor smaller than the bower often used with a fibre cable instead of a chain. Used for hauling a vessel off when she has gone aground.

Ketch—A fore and aft rigged vessel with two masts, a main and mizzen, the mizzen being stepped forward of the sternpost.

Lee shore—A shore down wind of a sailing vessel.

Lines—The shape of a vessel, as shown in the set of drawings comprising body plan, sheer plan, and half-breadth plan.

Loran—A system of radio navigation which relies on measuring the time difference between signals transmitted simultaneously from two shore stations.

Loxodromic—A straight line on a Mercator chart.

Mercator chart—A chart with a projection in which points of the compass preserve the same direction all over the map.

Monohull—A vessel with one hull.

Multihull—A vessel with more than one hull.

Off-course alarm—An electric alarm which sounds when the vessel goes off-course.

Pigs—Weights of lead used to hold splines in position.

Pilot chart—A chart which shows oceanographic and climatological data.

Planimeter—An instrument used to measure the area of irregular figures.

Radio beacon—A broadcasting station which sends out a signal so that bearings of it may be obtained with a radio set.

Ratlines—Horizontal ropes seized to a pair of shrouds to form a ladder in the rigging.

Reach—A point of sailing with the wind abeam or forward of the beam, but not so far forward as to make the vessel close-hauled.

Reef, to—To reduce the area of a sail by tying or rolling up a part of it.

R.O.R.C.—Royal Ocean Racing Club.

Rigging-screw—A fitting with threaded ends screwing into a common body; used for setting up the rigging.

Roller-reef—To reef a sail by winding it on to a boom.

Rudder stock—The part of a rudder which is closest to the sternpost.

Rumb line—A straight line on a Mercator chart.

Run, to—To sail before the wind.

Running rigging—Sheets, halliard, topping lifts, etc., by means of which sails are hoisted, trimmed, and controlled, as opposed to standing rigging which is a fixture.

Sausage skin—A lace-up canvas bag for stowing sails on deck.

Self-draining cockpit—A cockpit whose floor is above the level of the sea and which is fitted with draining holes.

Self-steering gear—A mechanism which corrects the vessel's heading when it wanders off course.

Sheer—The curve of the gunwale seen in profile.

Short-wave converter—An attachment on the radio receiver which allows tuning to lower frequencies.

Shrouds—Wire ropes giving athwartships support to a mast, bowsprit or bumkin.

Sloop—A fore and aft rigged vessel with one mast, a mainsail and one head-sail.

Spinnaker—A triangular sail set on the opposite side to the mainsail when a vessel is running.

Spline—A thin strip of wood or plastic used to draw a curved line.

Spreaders—Wood or metal struts on a mast to give the rigging more spread. Usually called crosstrees.

Stanchion—A support for bulwarks, guardrails, etc.

Standard rigging—Shrouds, stays, etc., which support the mast or some other spar, and are not handled in the sailing of the vessel.

Stiff—A vessel is said to be stiff when she does not readily heel. The opposite to crank or tender.

Tack—The lower forward corner of a sail. Also to sail as close to the wind as the vessel will go with advantage.

Tackle—A purchase formed by the combination of a rope with two or more blocks to give increased power.

Tang—A metal fitting screwed or bolted to a mast or spar for the attachment of rigging.

Topside That part of a vessel's side which is above water when she is afloat but not heeled.

Trimaran—A vessel with a float at each side of the main hull.

Waterlines—Horizontal sections of a vessel's hull at and below the waterline; seen as curves on the half-breadth plan.

Warp—Originally a strong rope by means of which a vessel was moved in or out of dock. The fibre rope attached to a kedge anchor is generally known as a kedge warp.

Weather helm—The tug of the tiller, away from the windward side of the boat.

Windward Shore—The shore to windward of the vessel.

Woven roving—Glassfibre which is woven like a cloth.

Yawl—A fore and aft rigged vessel with two masts, a main and mizzen, the mizzen being stepped aft of the sternpost.

Index

McKee, Paul, 58
Mashford, Sid, and Mashford's boat-
    yard, 63, 64, 67, 71, 79
Meteorological Office, 56, 58
Mid-Atlantic (June 9–13), 91–102;
    radio telephone calls, 91–3, 96–7;
    fog, 91; North Atlantic drift, 91;
    eating habits, 91–2; *Sir Thomas
    Lipton* escapes the deep depression,
    93; nearly overboard, 94, 96;
    navigational error, 98; reception
    of Canadian radio stations, 99; 'on
    days' and 'off days', 99; storm
    warning, 102
Model Racing Yachts (Priest and
    Lewis), 19
Moore, Dick, 58, 76, 89, 92
Muesel, Bill, 142
Mylor, 5–6, 11, 18, 53
Mystery, 26
Myth of Malham (Noel Bevan), 69,
    74–5, 131, 134, 160

Nantucket, 123, 126, 129, 142; con-
    solan, 108; Island, 126; Shoals,
    141–4
Nantucket Light Vessel, 123, 126,
    128–9, 141, 142; moved farther
    south, 129
New York, 7–10, 14, 19; Central
    Library, 9, 19; St. Bernard's
    School, 7, 20, 22, 149
Newfoundland, 110; ground wave
    signals, 107. *See also* Grand Banks
Newport, 89, 132, 134, 135, 140–2,
    146, 150, 152; Castle Hill coast-
    guard station, 142, 144, 146; *Sir
    Thomas Lipton's* position reported
    to, 142, 144, 146; reception of *Sir
    Thomas Lipton*, 148; arrival at fin-
    ishing line at Brenton Tower, 148

Nomans Island, 144
North Atlantic drift, 91
North Cornish coast, 1, 3–4, 154
Nova Scotia shore, 126, 132

Observer, The: sponsors 1960 Trans-
    atlantic Race, 9; weather forecasts,
    102
Ocean Highlander, 69, 161
Ocean Youth Club, 154
Odling-Smee, Lt.-Col., 142–3
Outward Bound projects, 154
Oxford University, 115–17; Expedi-
    tion to Northern Persia, 7, 11, 91,
    140; St. Edmund Hall, 6

Pen-Duick III, 11, 14, 24, 36, 162
Pen-Duick IV (Eric Tabarly), 69, 71,
    128; sail plan, 72; specifications, 72;
    arrangement, 73
Pendennis Point, 51, 53
Perkins, John, 44
Philip, Prince: President of Royal
    Yachting Association, 21; views on
    sponsorship, 21
Pirelli webbing berths, 32, 84
Plasticell non-porous foam, 18, 19,
    24, 34, 37
Plymouth, 122, 130, 147; *Sir Thomas
    Lipton* arrives for Race, 63; com-
    peting boats in Millbay Docks, 63;
    start of Race, 66–9; Ocean Youth
    Club, 154

Qualifying passage, five hundred
    miles, 49–55; in Solent, 49; to the
    Barfleur light, 50; tacking to west-
    ward, 50; turning point west of
    Ushant, 50; voyage to Falmouth,
    50–4; halliard jams off Pendennis
    Point, 51; attempts to cut down
    sail, 51–2; manoeuvring to the

172

Qualifying—*Contd.*
North Bank, 53–4; anchoring, 54; damaged fingers, 54–5; fastest qualifying time, 55

Radio Halifax, 134
Radio St. John (Newfoundland), 102
Radio transmitter, 61
Rame Head, 63, 69
Raph (Alain Gliksman), 69, 71, 83, 93, 100, 131, 161; most feared competitor, 64; longest monohull entered, 64; arrangements, 81; sail plan, 80; specifications, 80; retired from Race, 134; track chart, 168–70
Redruth, 1–3, 152
Redwing dinghies, 7, 116
Resin, 24, 35, 37
Restronguet Sailing Club, 7
Richborough Wharf, 39, 41
Rig, 14, 27–31; influence of weather, 27; twin running sails, 31
Rob Roy, 70, 160
Round Britain Race, 18, 151
Roundabout, 24
Royal Military Academy, Sandhurst, sails *Sir Thomas Lipton* home, 152–3
Royal Ocean Racing Club (R.O.R.C.), 10; Duarnenez race (1967), 24; championship (1968), 26; rating rules, 32; ocean races, 56, 131
Royal Western Yacht Club, 9
Royal Yachting Association, 21
Running sails, twin, 31

Sable Island, 123, 126
Sail area, 14, 16
Sail plan, 28

St. Bernard's School, New York, 7, 20, 22, 149; sail training ventures, 7–8, 21, 149
Sandwich, Kent, 34, 38–40
Sandwich method, *see* Foam core method
Scillies, the, 75, 112, 122
Sea Spirit, 26
Self-steering gear ('the Colonel'), 11, 45–6, 50, 114, 137
Seth-Smith, Commander David, 24
Seven Pillars of Wisdom, The (Lawrence), 110
Shamrocks (Sir Thomas Lipton's yachts), 23, 40
Silvia II (André Foezon), 68, 160
Sir Thomas Lipton: name of boat, 23; thinking behind boat, 26–33; rig, 27–31; sail plan, 28–9, 31; specifications, 28; arrangement, 29; hull shape, 31–2; building, 34–42; trials, 42–55; computer navigation, 21–2, 56–62, 87, 111–13, 123; radio transmitter, 61; analysis of sail changes and conditions, 158–9; track charts, 168–70
Size of singlehander's boat, 15, 27
Slater, Ian, 58, 89
Snelling, Mr., names *Sir Thomas Lipton*, 40
Solent, the, 44, 46, 49
Specifications for *Sir Thomas Lipton*, 28
Speed graphs, 60
Spirit of Cutty Sark (Leslie Williams), 69, 100, 160; arrangements, 95; sail plan, 94; specifications, 94; track chart, 168–70
Sponsorship, 11–12, 15, 16, 19–24; Allied Suppliers' offer, 23; Prince Philip's view, 21